Great Grandkids

Volume 2

By Dr. Jay Charles Soper

This book is dedicated to
Uncle Jimmy and Aunt Jan.
Thanks for making Harry and Laura so happy!

Great Grandkids Volume 2

By Dr. Jay Charles Soper

© Jay Charles Soper, 2013

All rights reserved.

ISBN-13: 978-1494389697

ISBN-10: 149438969X

BISAC category: Photography / Subjects & Themes / Children

Published in the USA by CreateSpace.com

Introduction to Volume 2 of *Great Grandkids*

"Being a parent is one of life's great joys," or so I'd heard. Now that I've experienced it in my own skin for 9 years, I can testify that it is true.

I'm happy to share some of our most joyous moments. Herein you'll find pictures of year 2 of Harry Daniel (November 2005-October 2006) and Laura Susanna Soper (November 2012-October 2013).

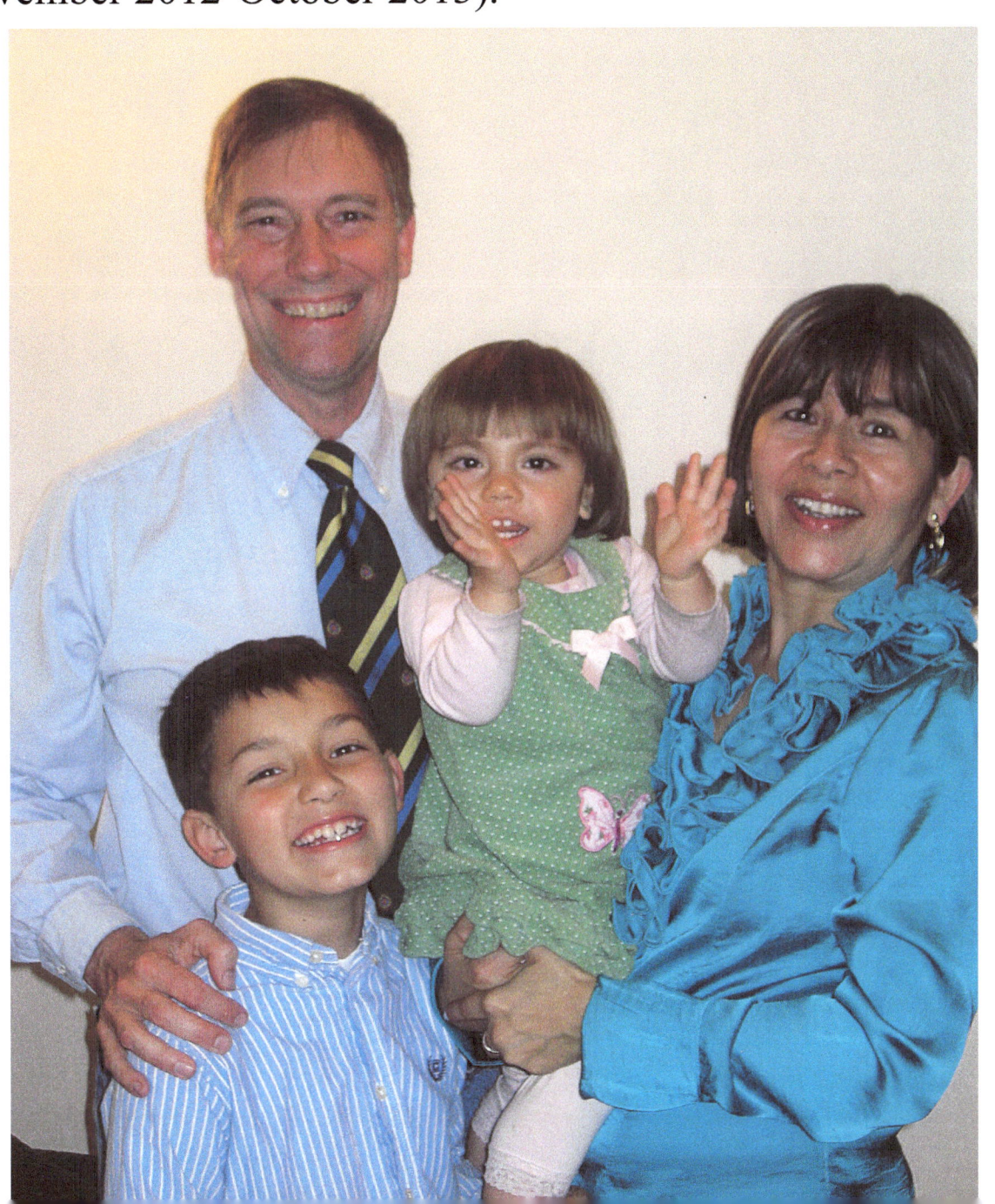

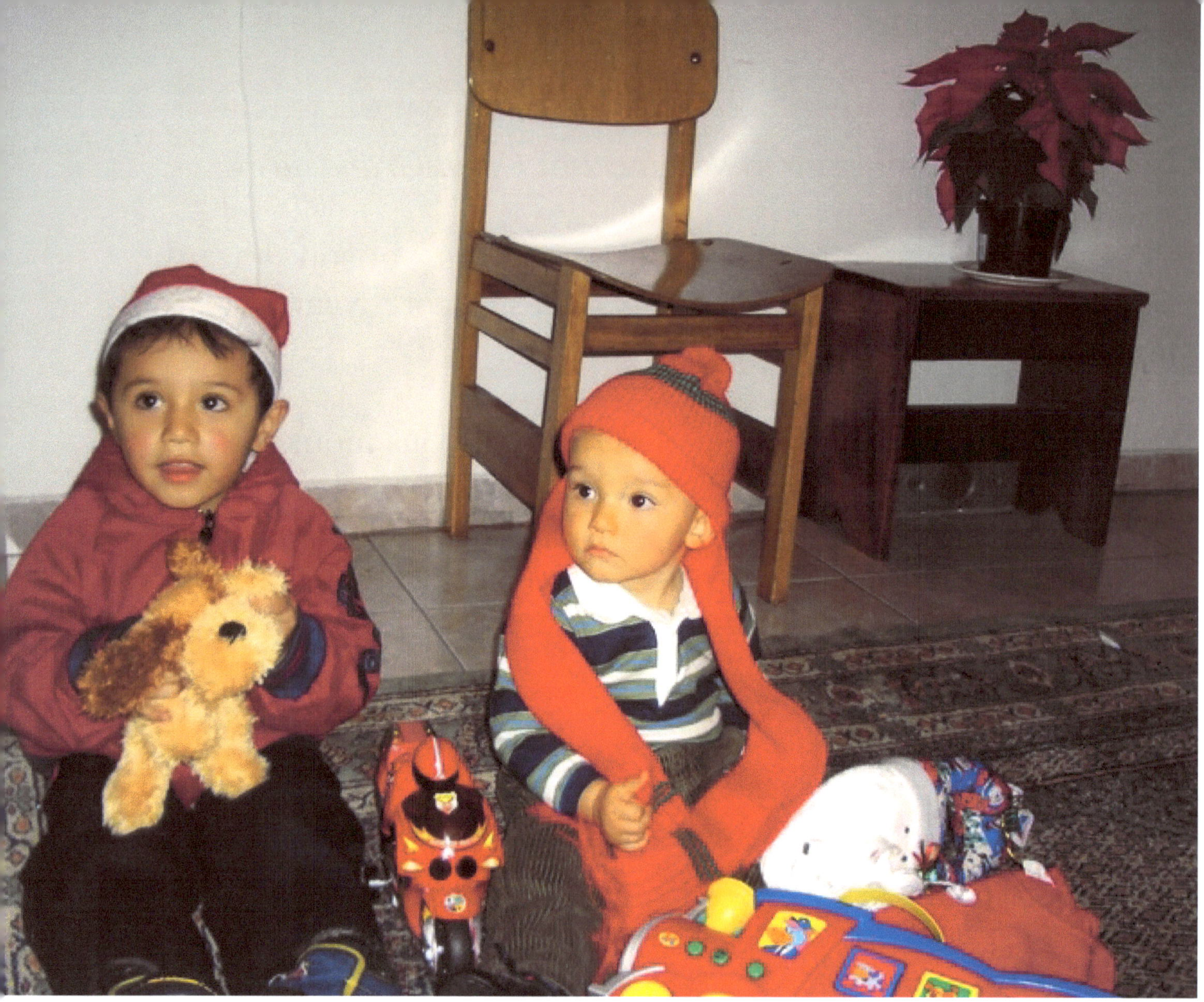

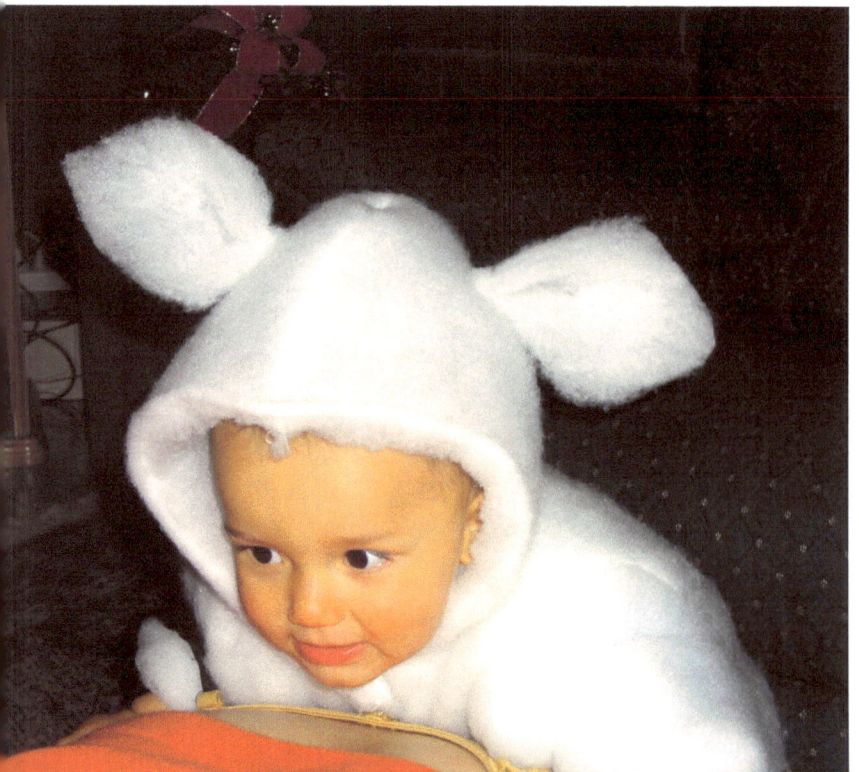

Harry Daniel and his friend Sebastian are ready for Christmas.

Shepherd Ruth carries her little sheep for Philadelphia Church's Christmas program.

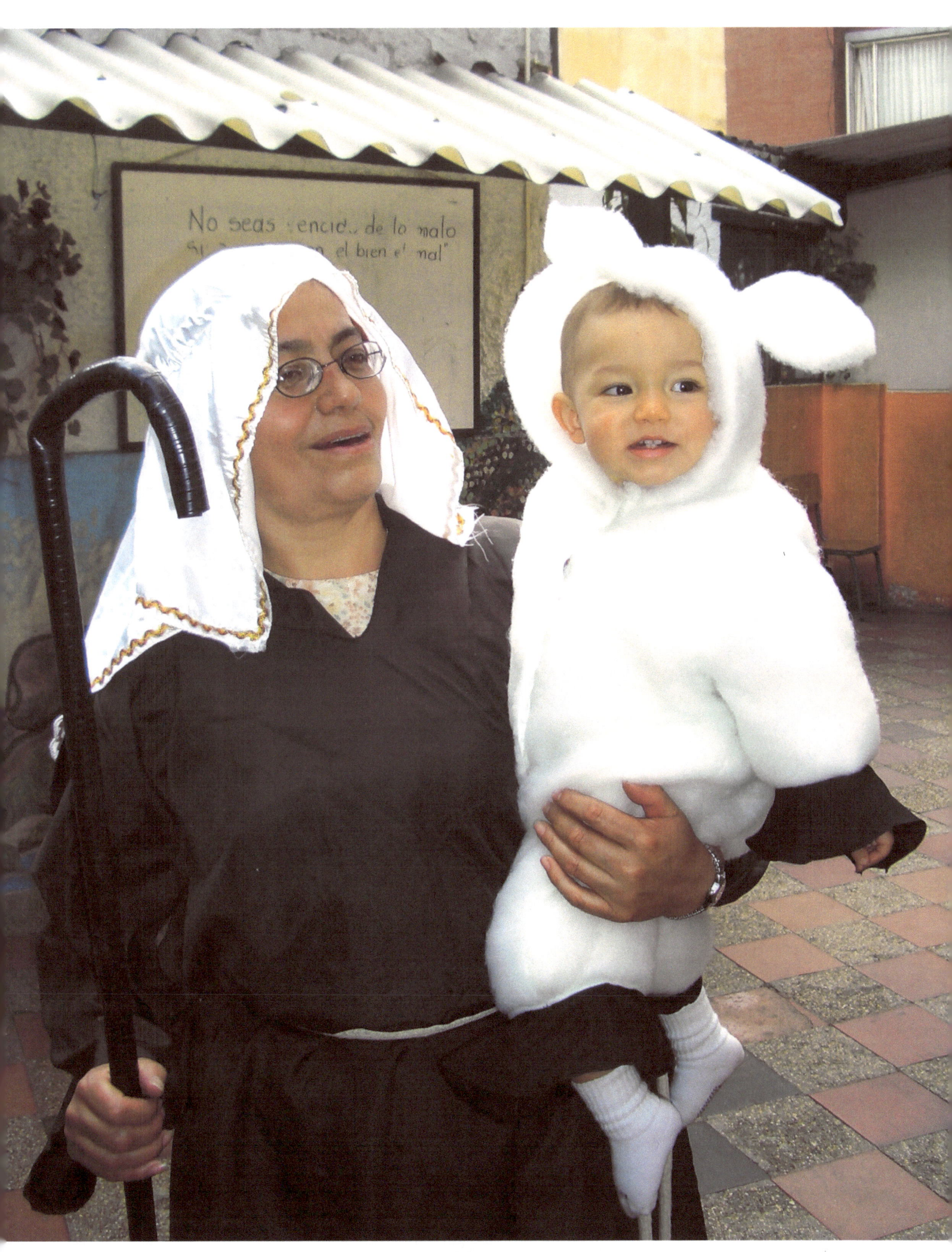

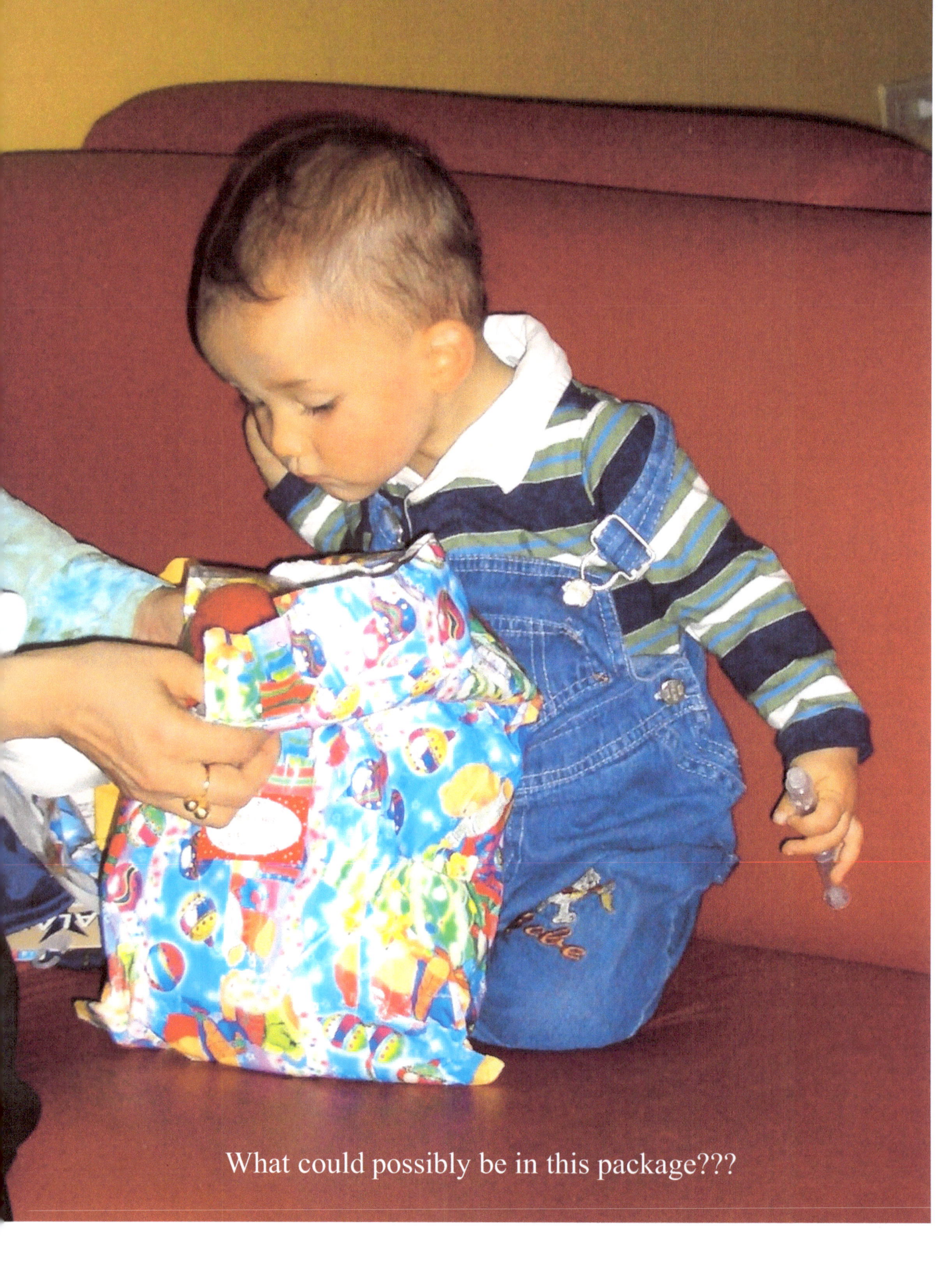

What could possibly be in this package???

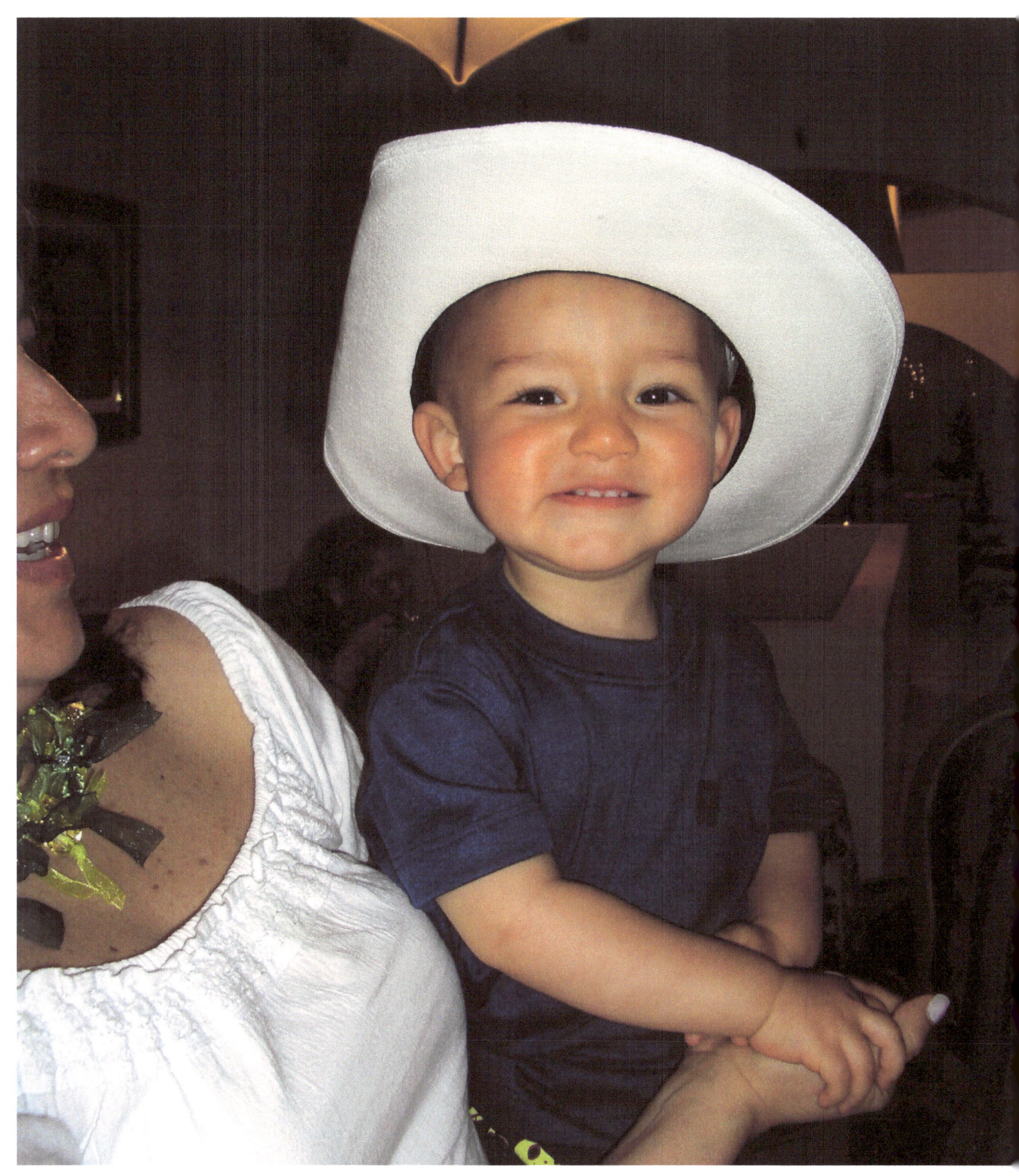

Christmas was so much fun!

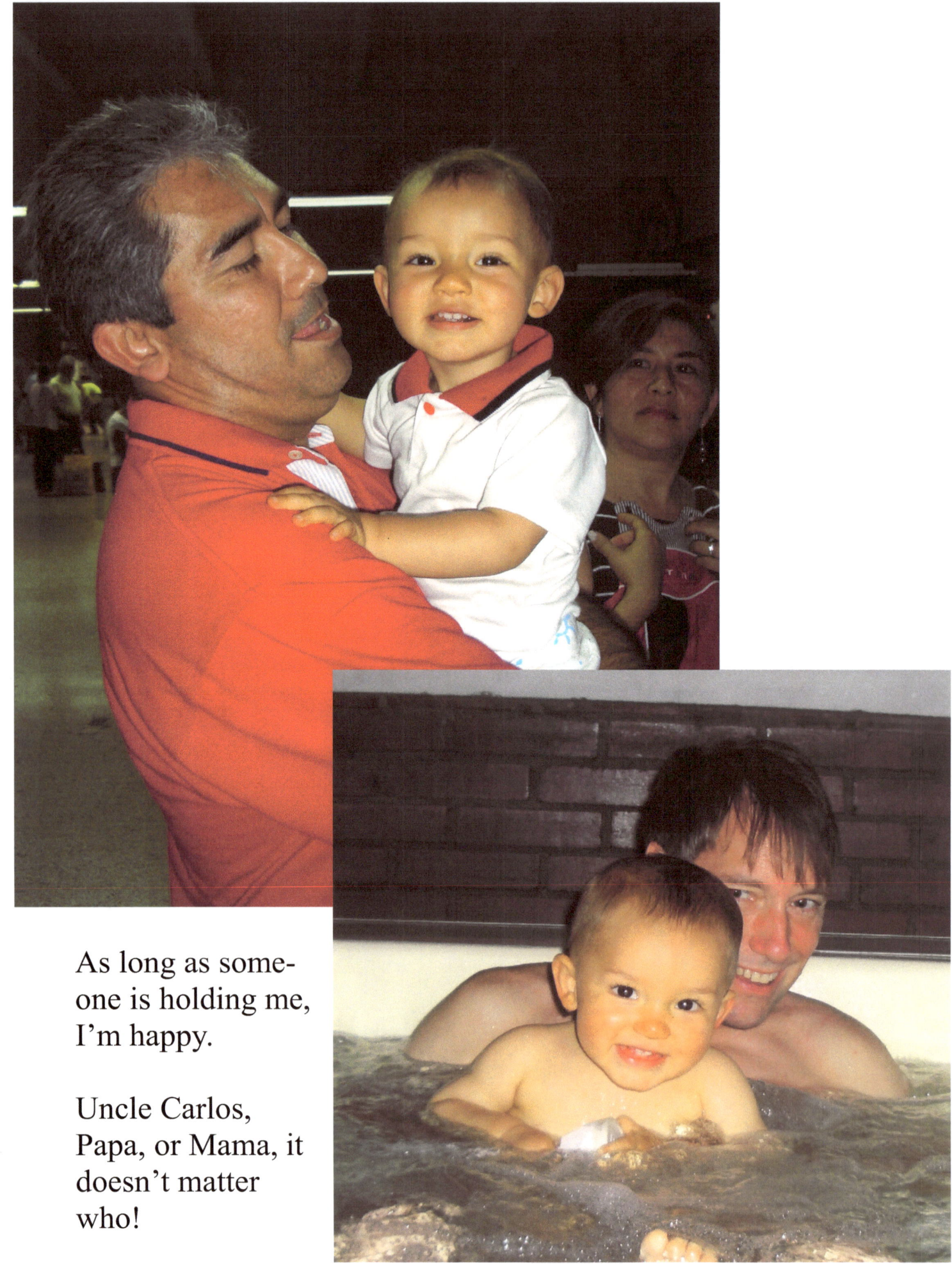

As long as some-
one is holding me,
I'm happy.

Uncle Carlos,
Papa, or Mama, it
doesn't matter
who!

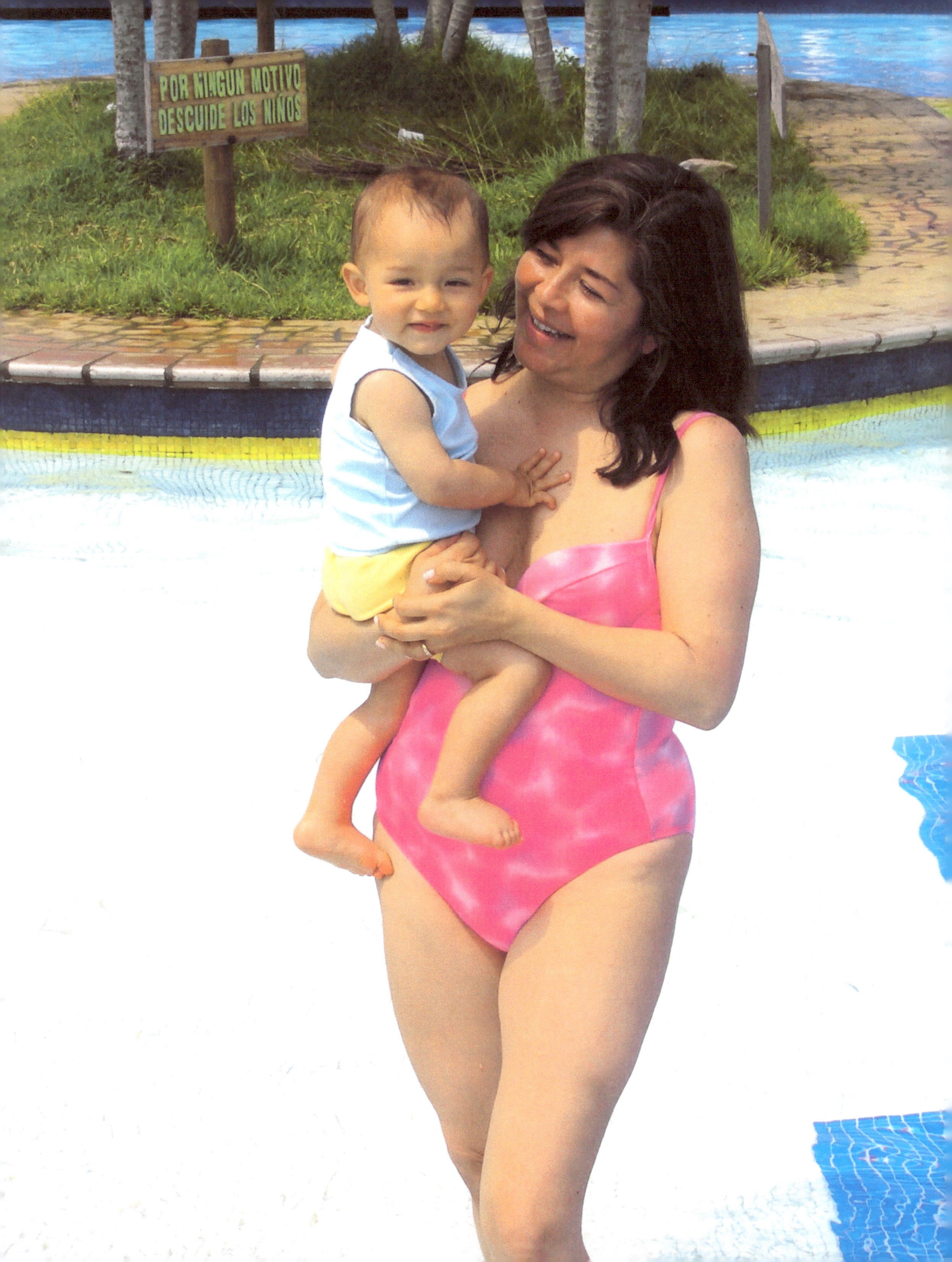

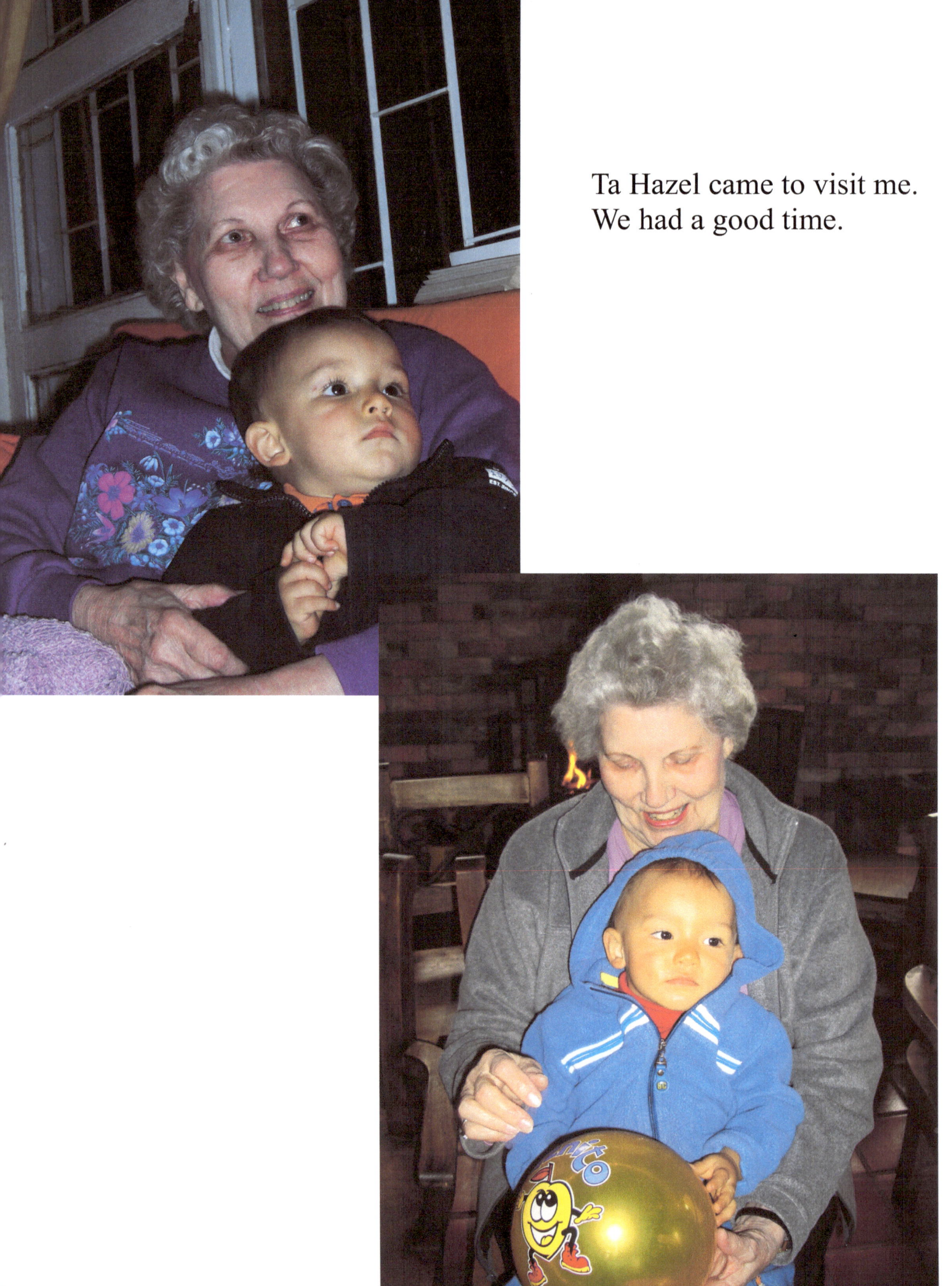

Ta Hazel came to visit me.
We had a good time.

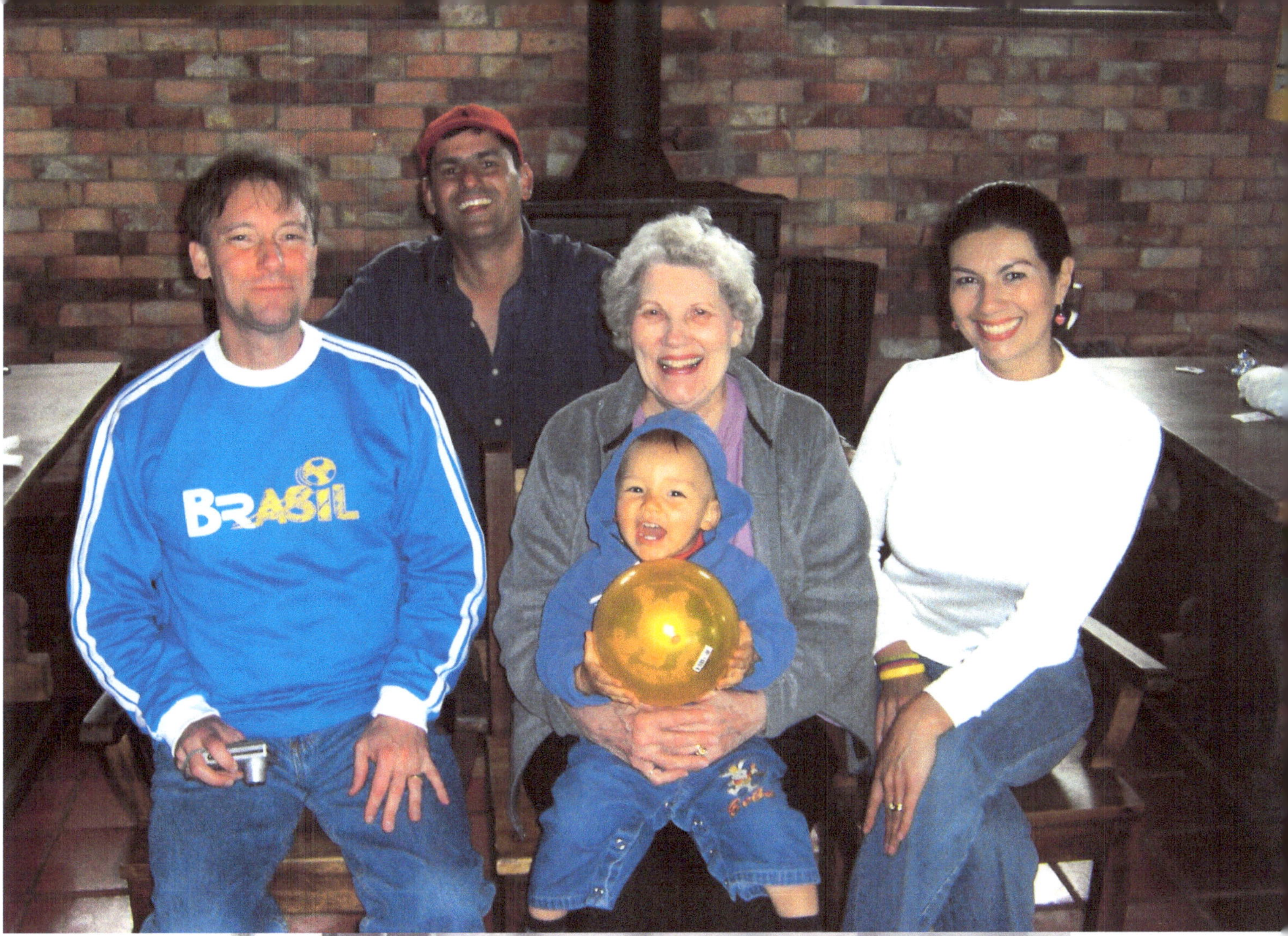

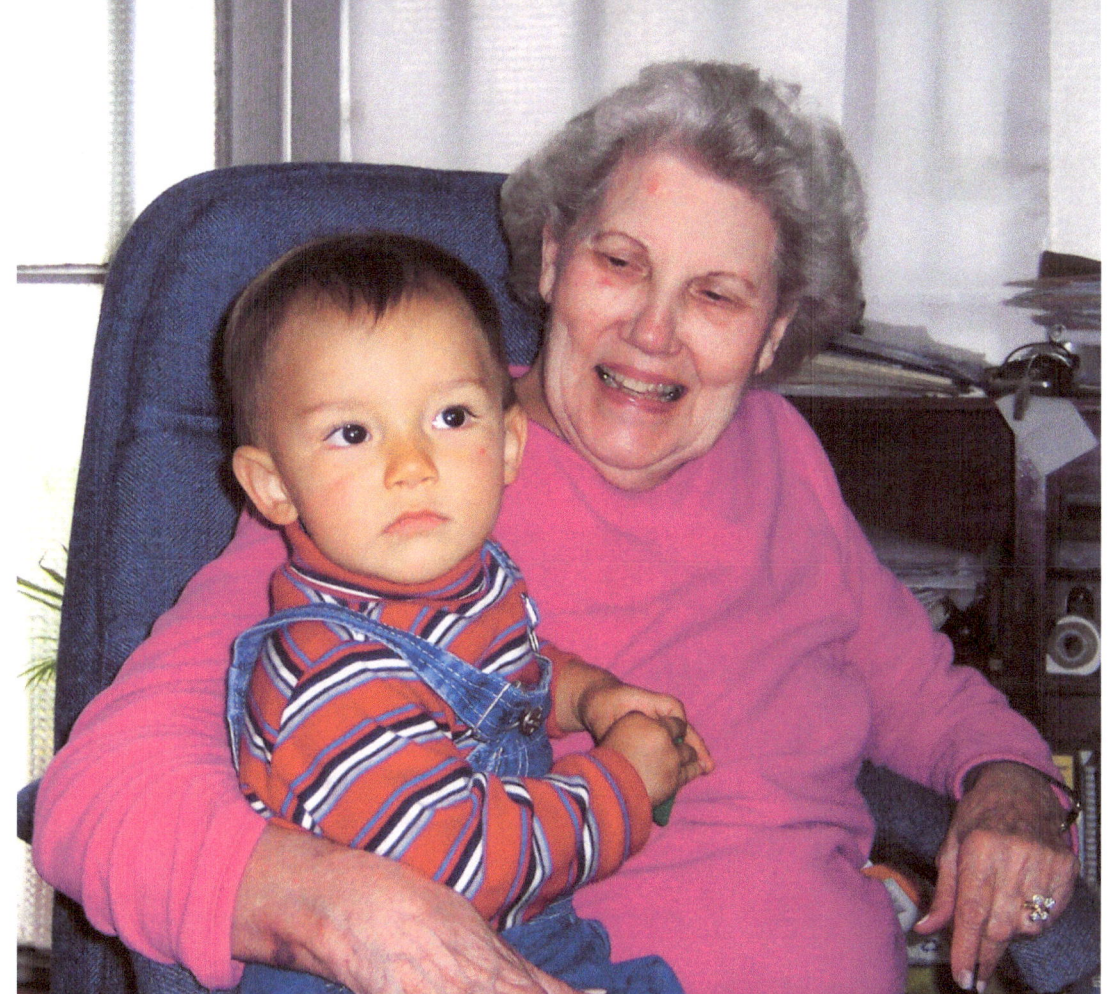

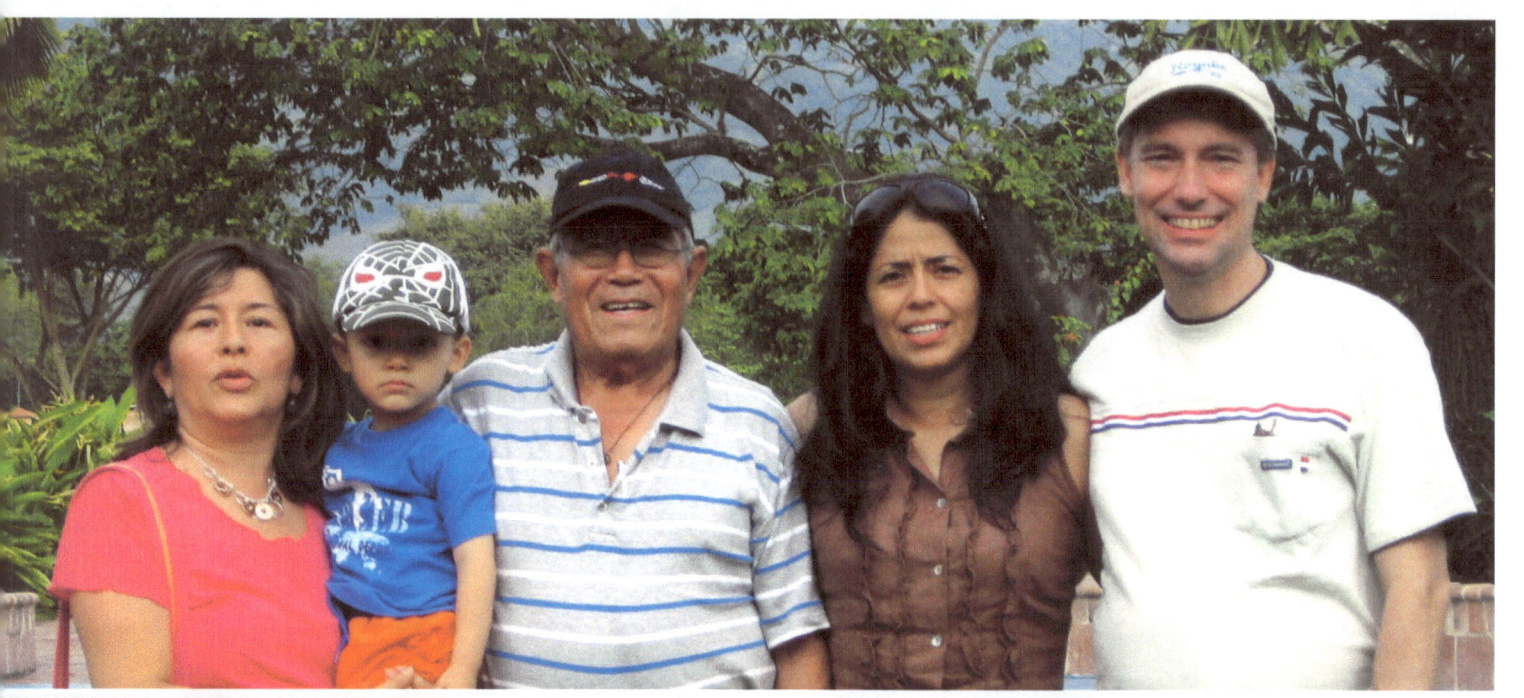

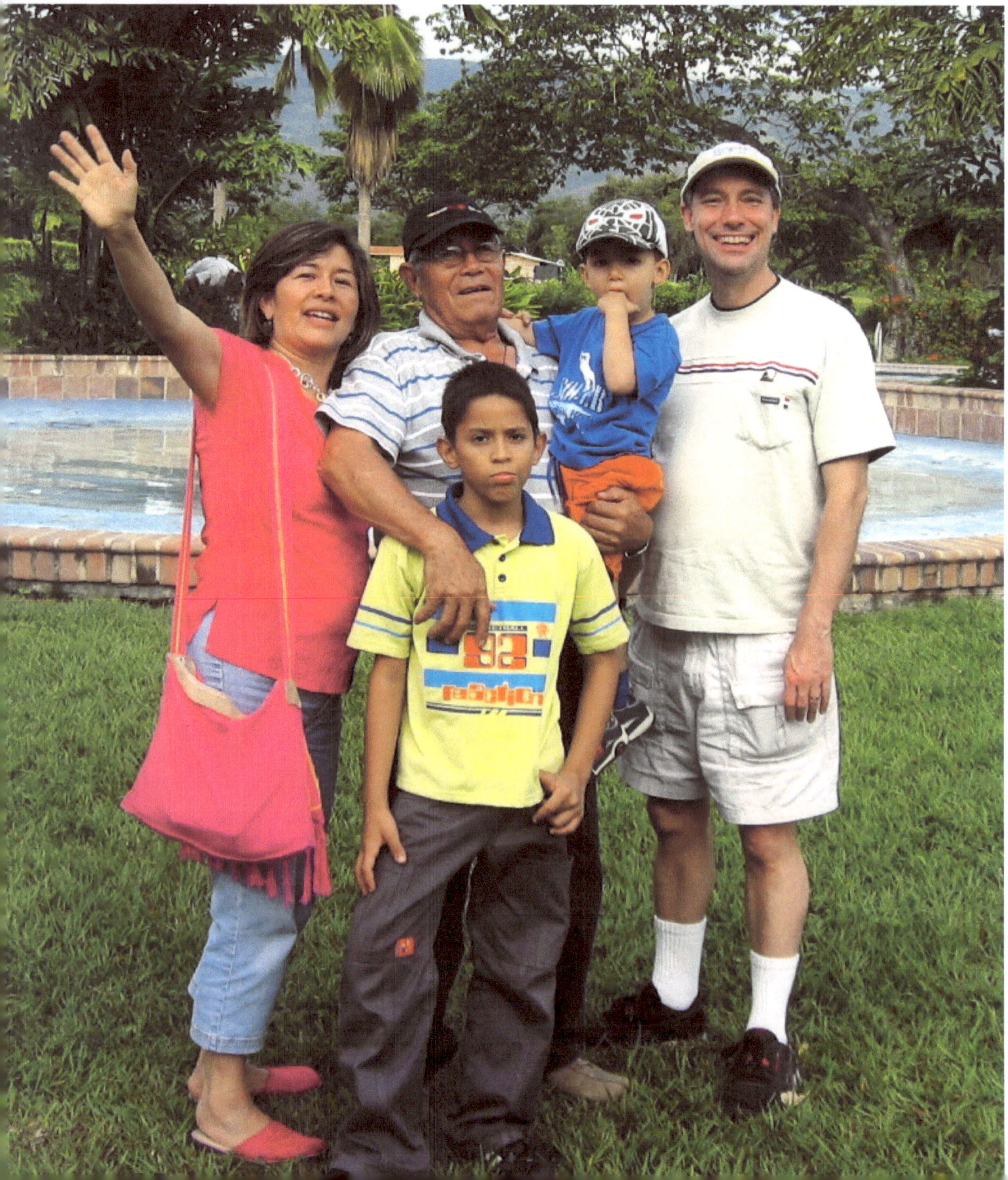

Here I am with Grandpa Ulpiano, Aunt Marleny, and Cousin Sebastian.

Don't I look cute in my baseball cap?

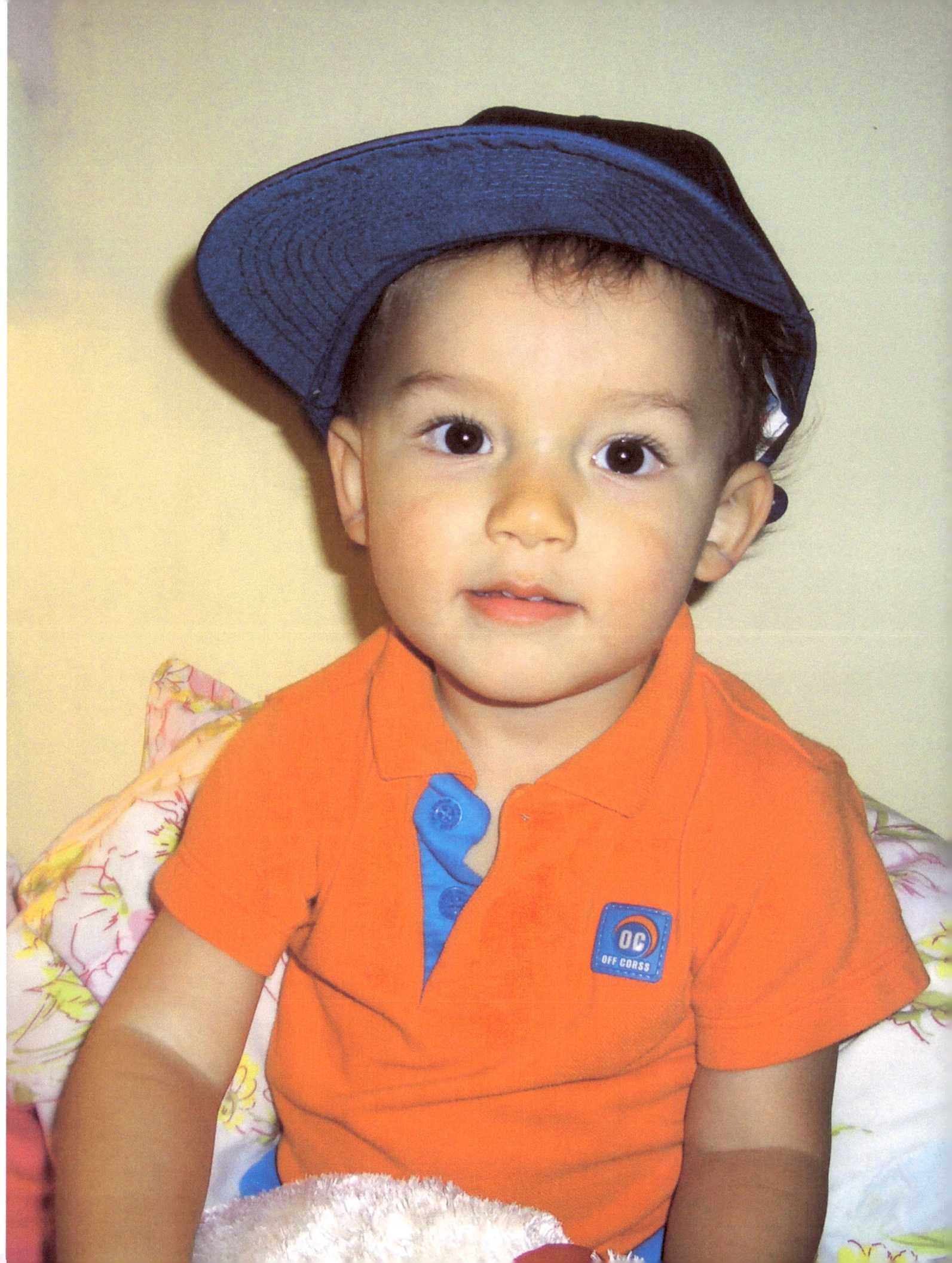

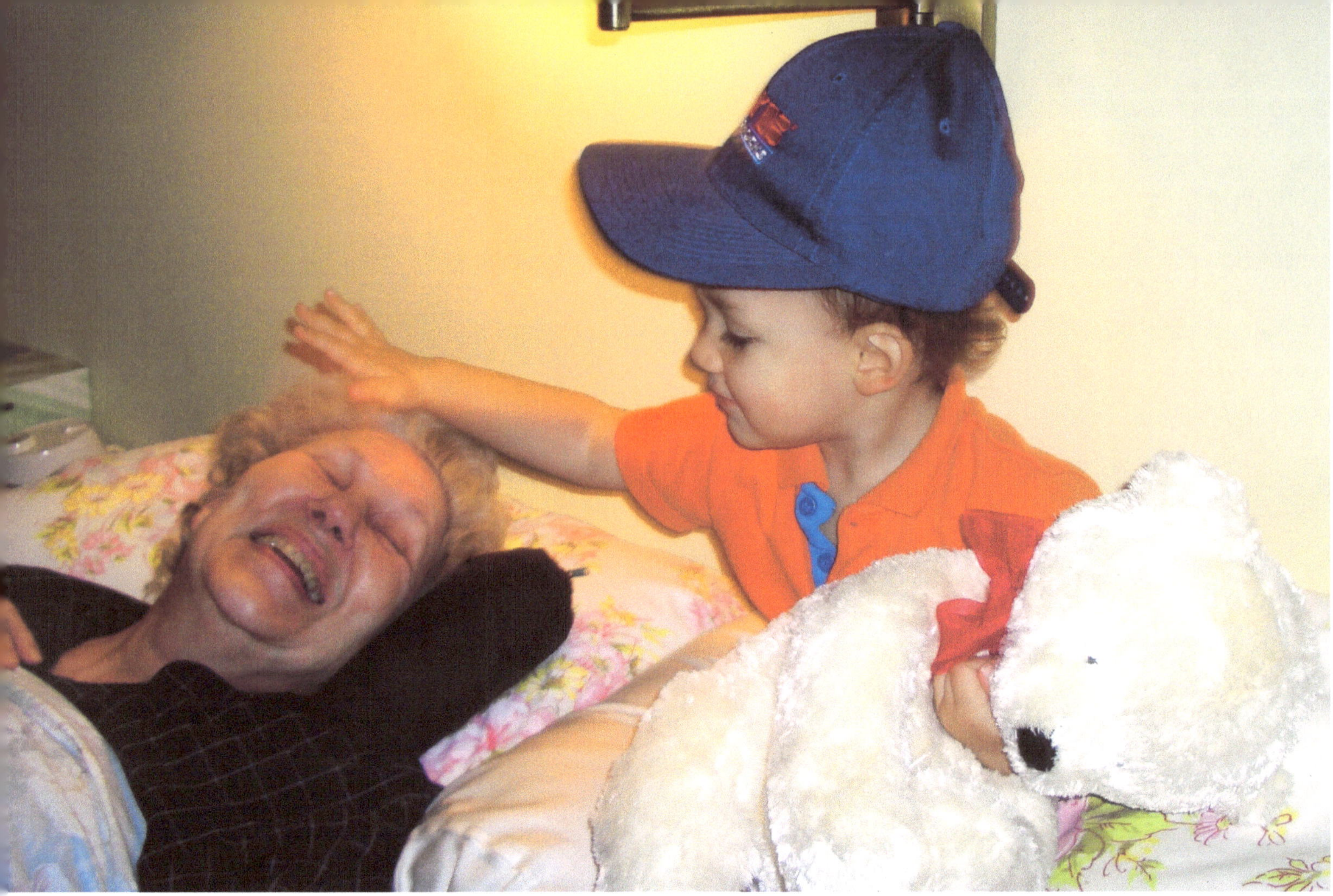

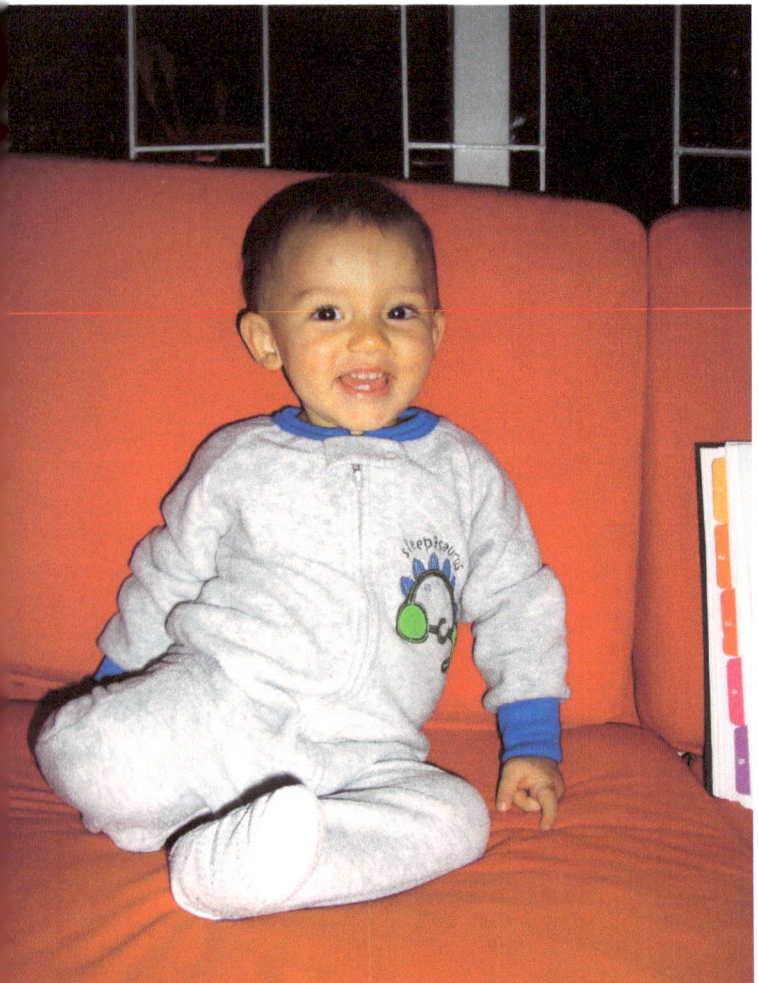

Ta Hazel looks like she needs a pat on the head.

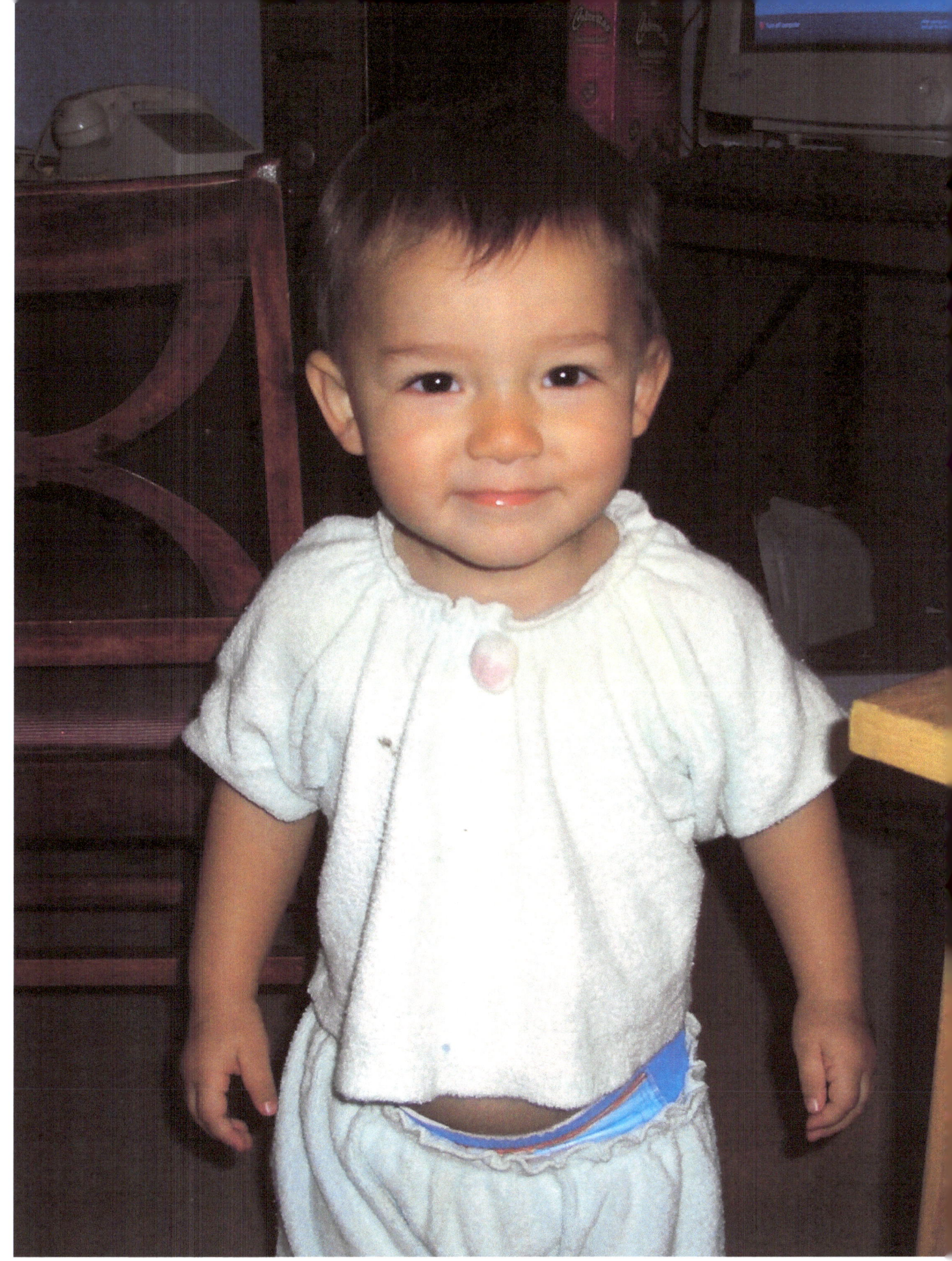

I think these pajamas used to be my papa's!

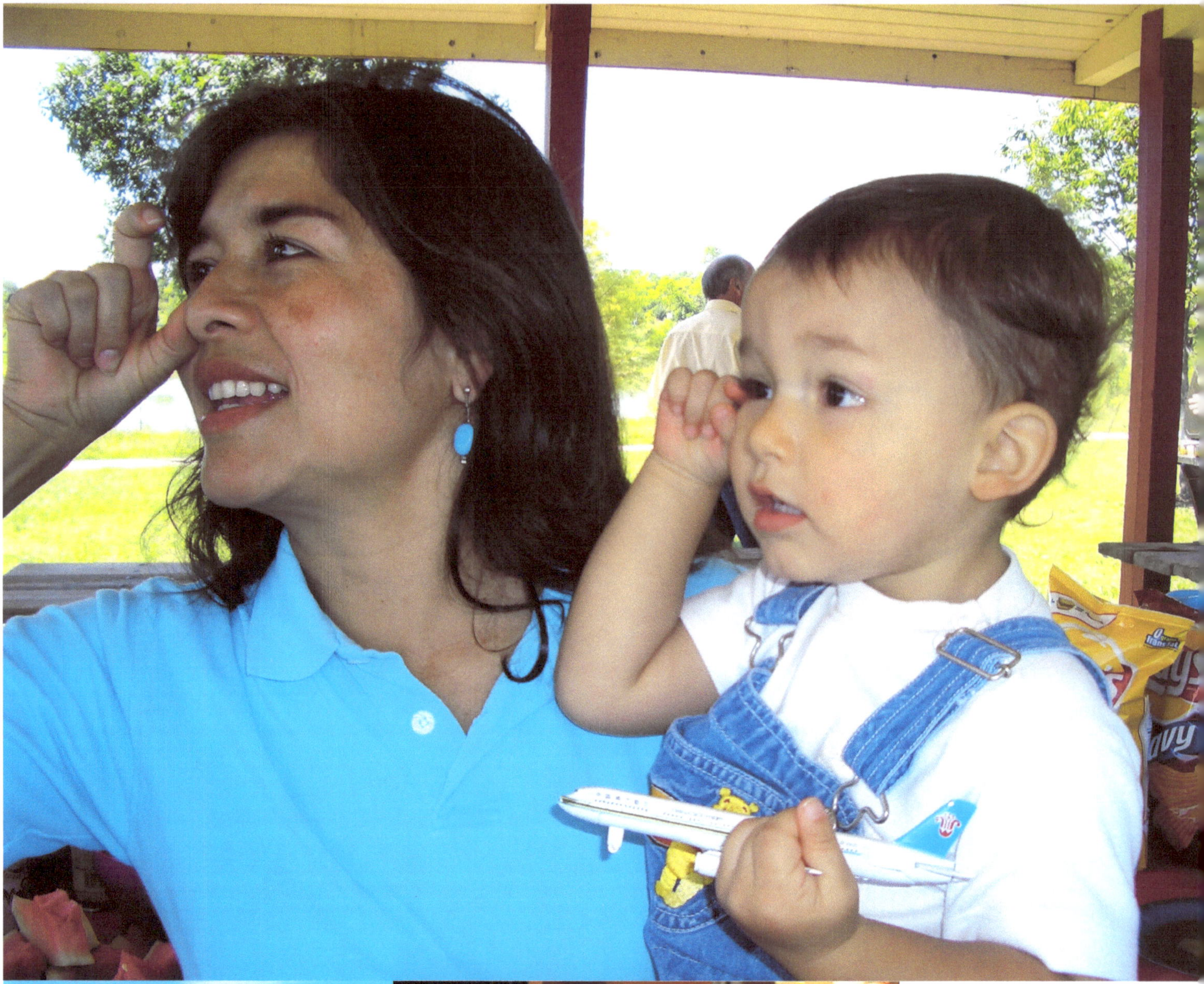

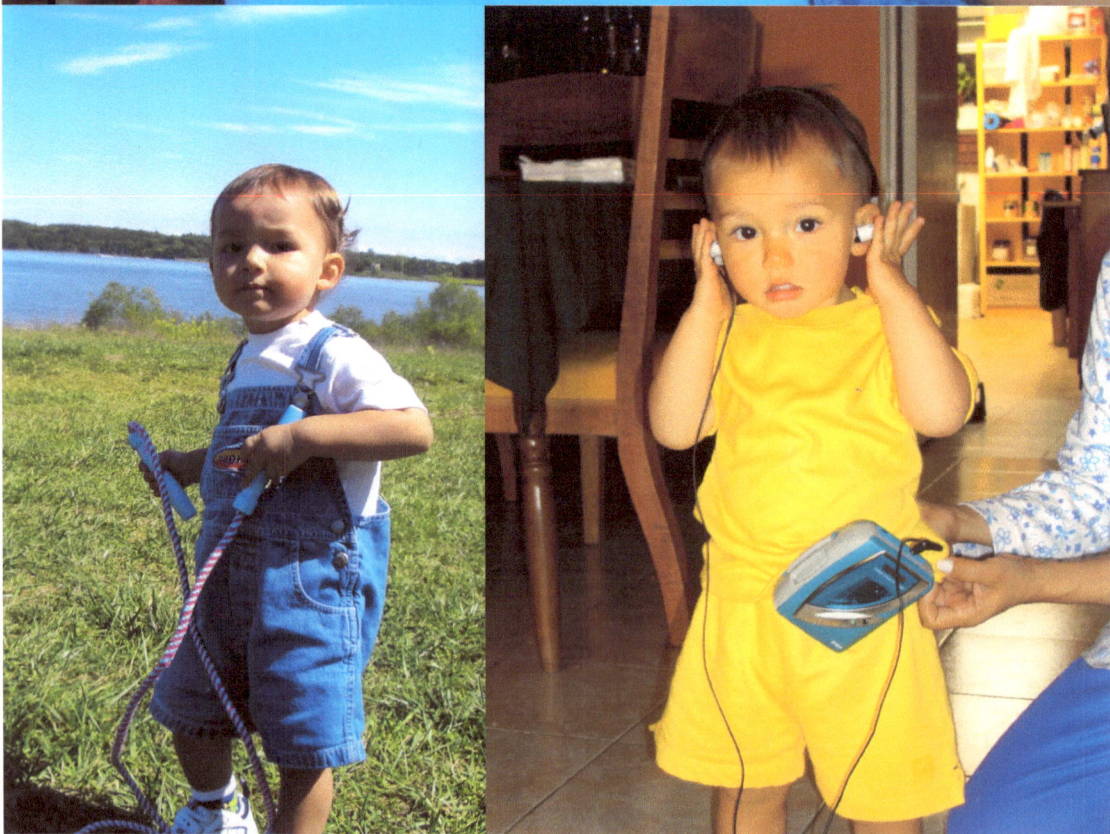

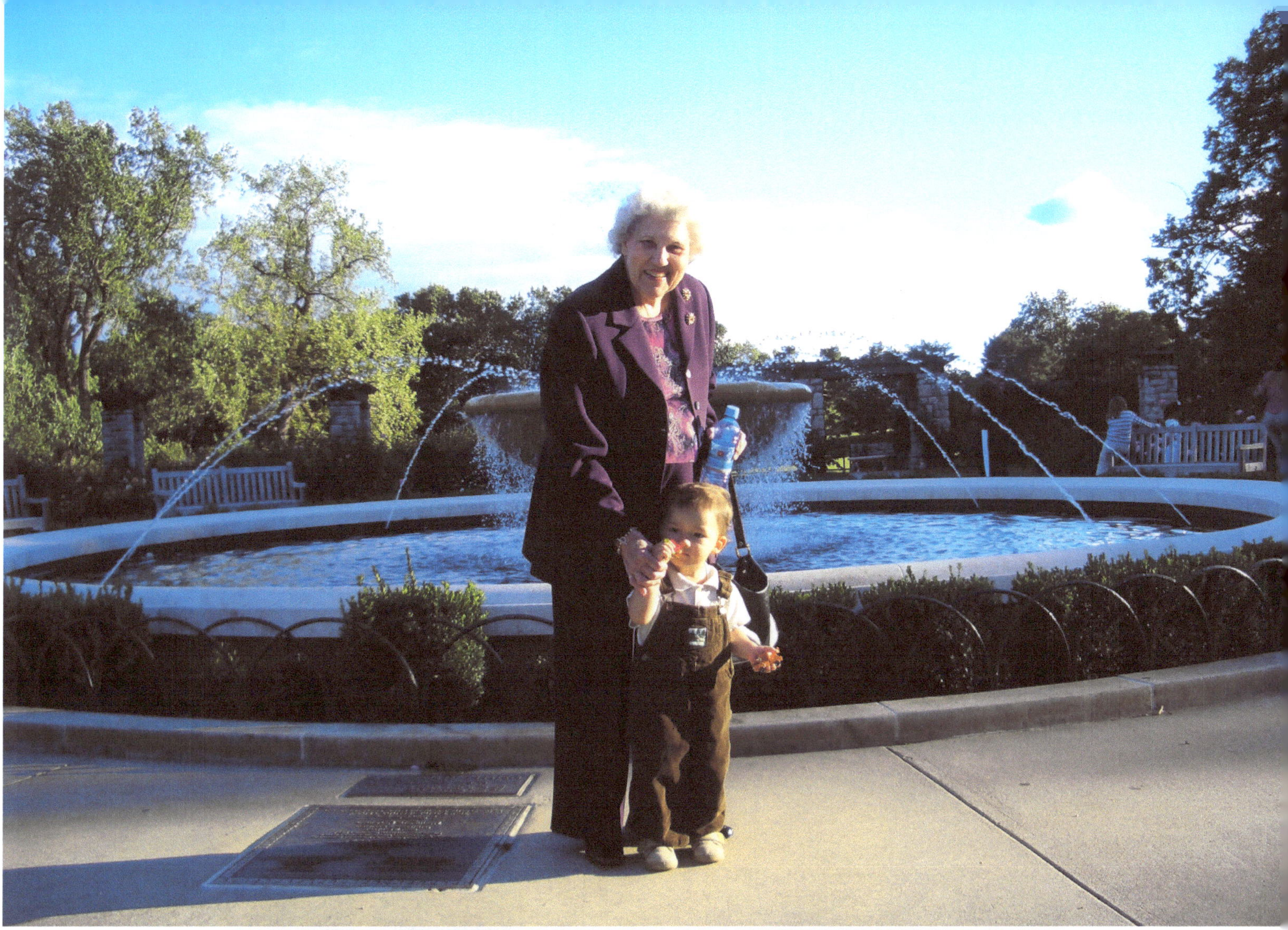

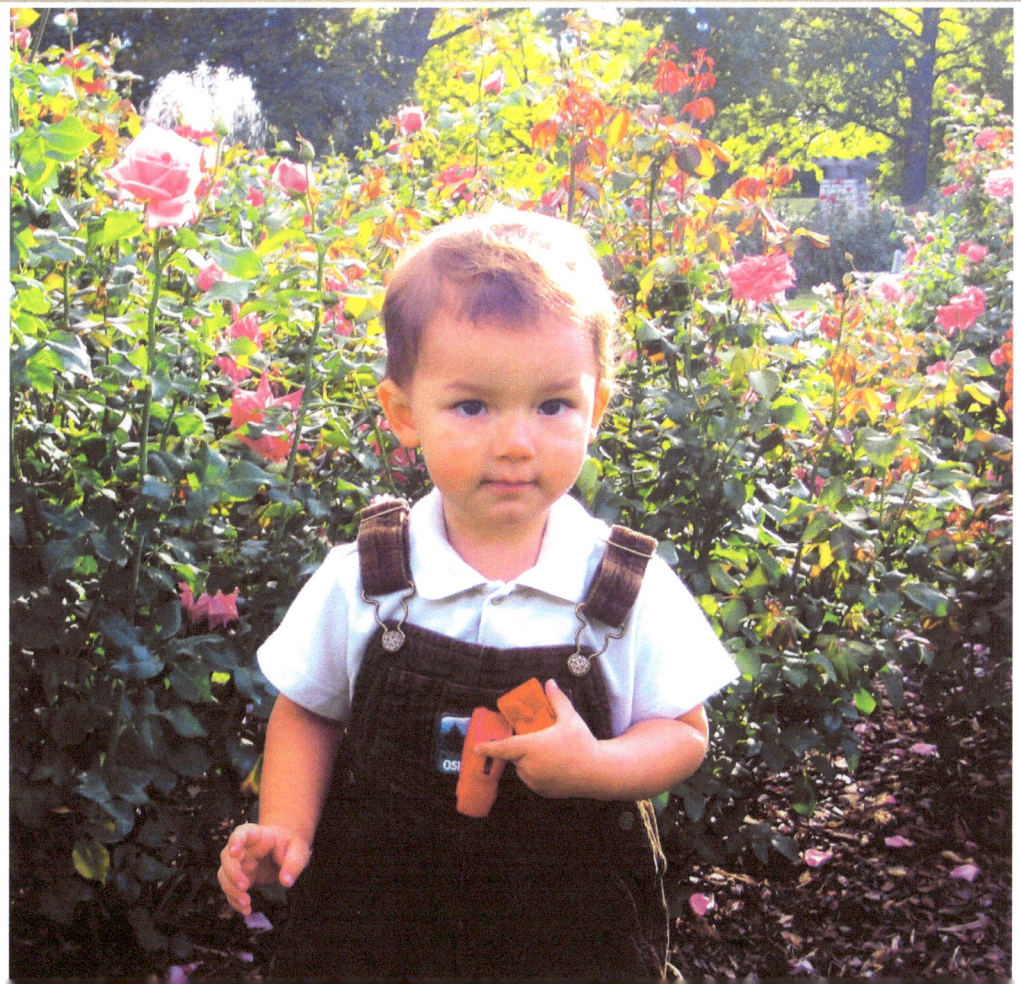

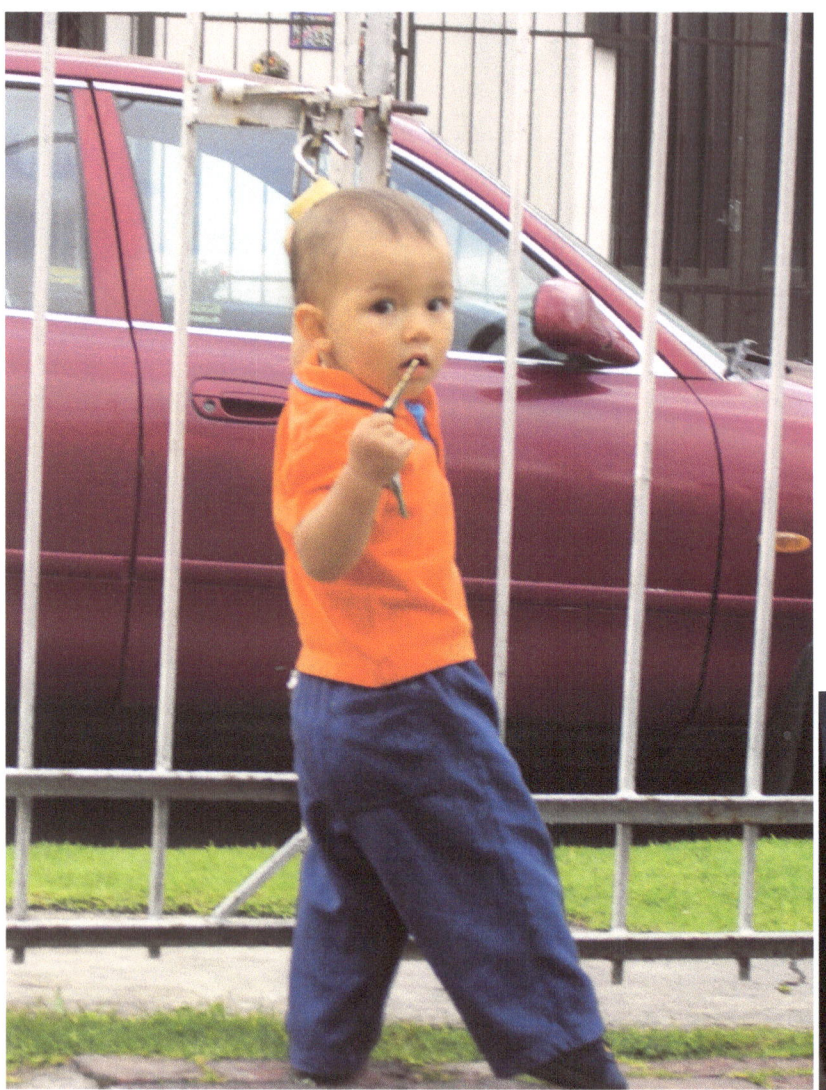

I just love hearing the car go "beep" when I touch this button.

Papa's shoes are still a little big for me.

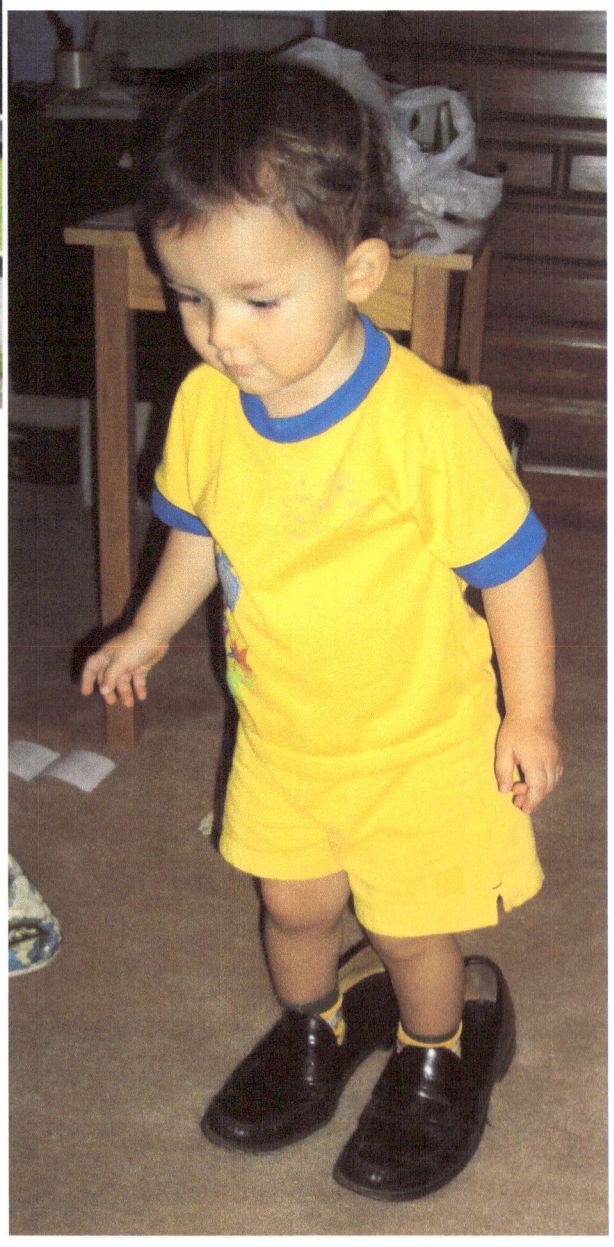

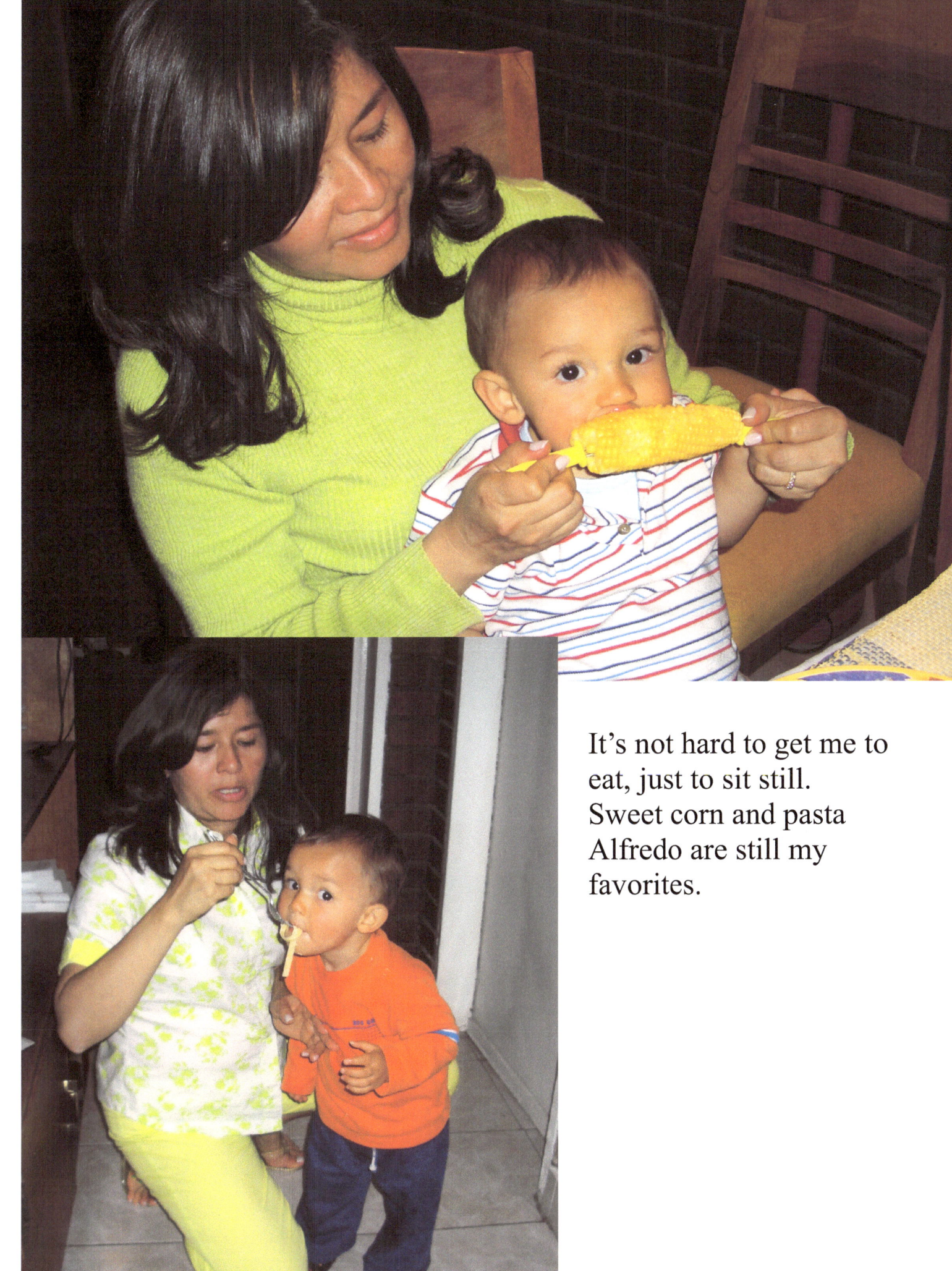

It's not hard to get me to eat, just to sit still. Sweet corn and pasta Alfredo are still my favorites.

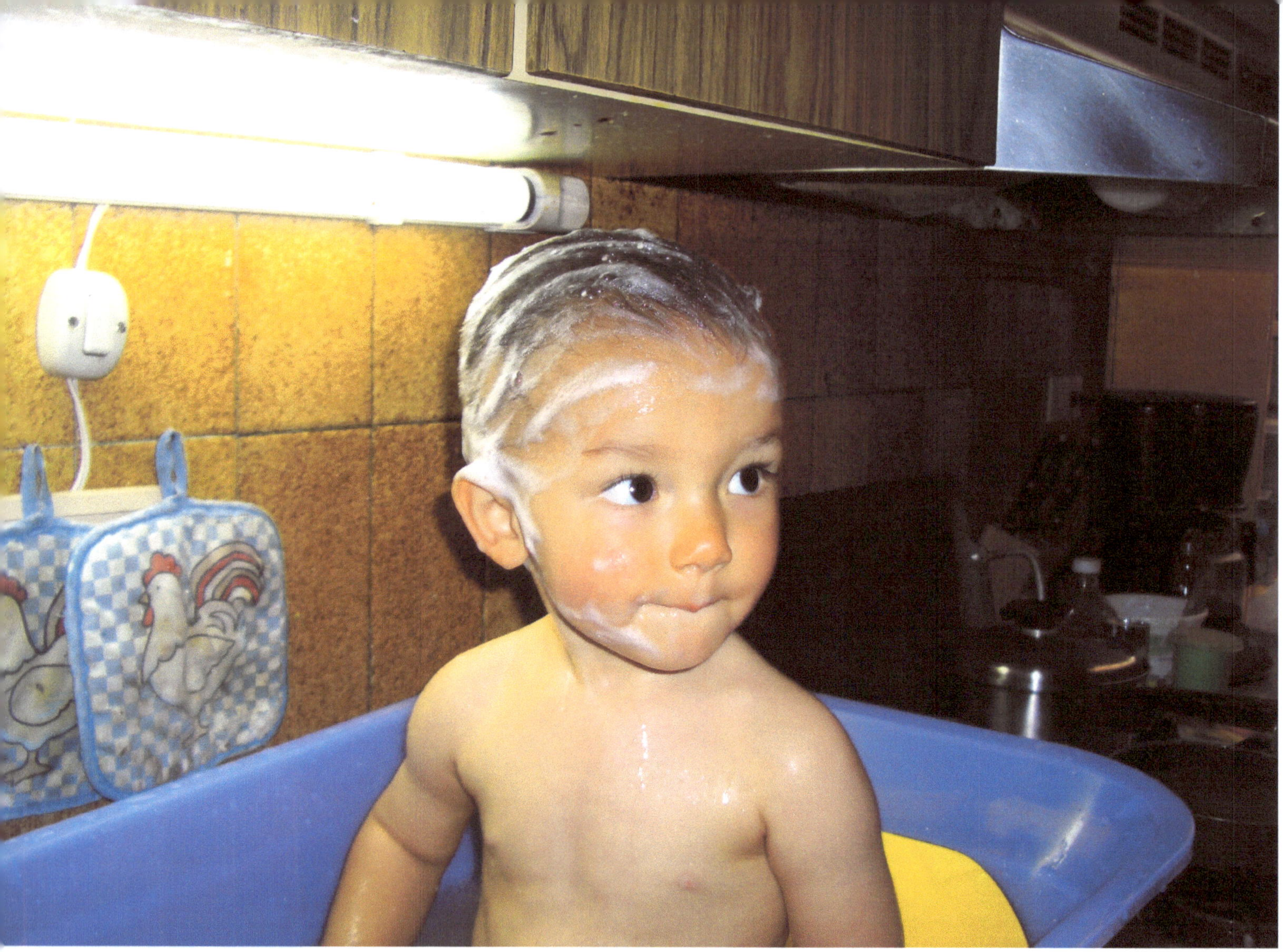

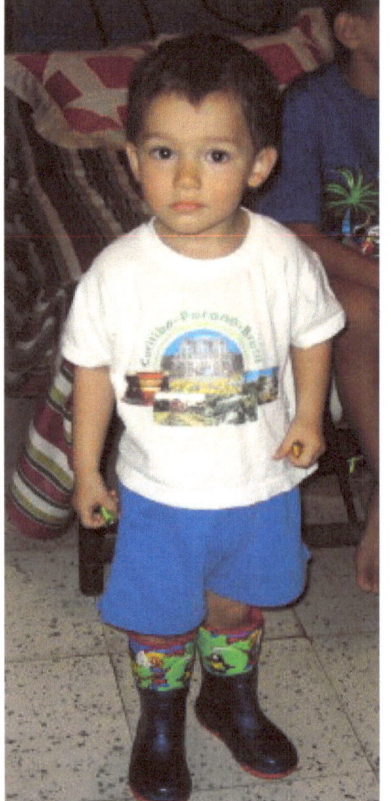

Brocoli is good!

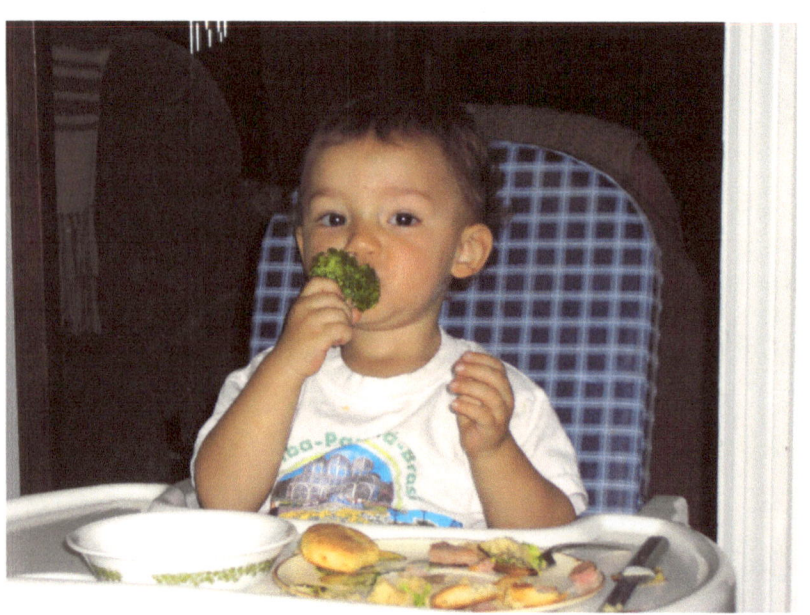

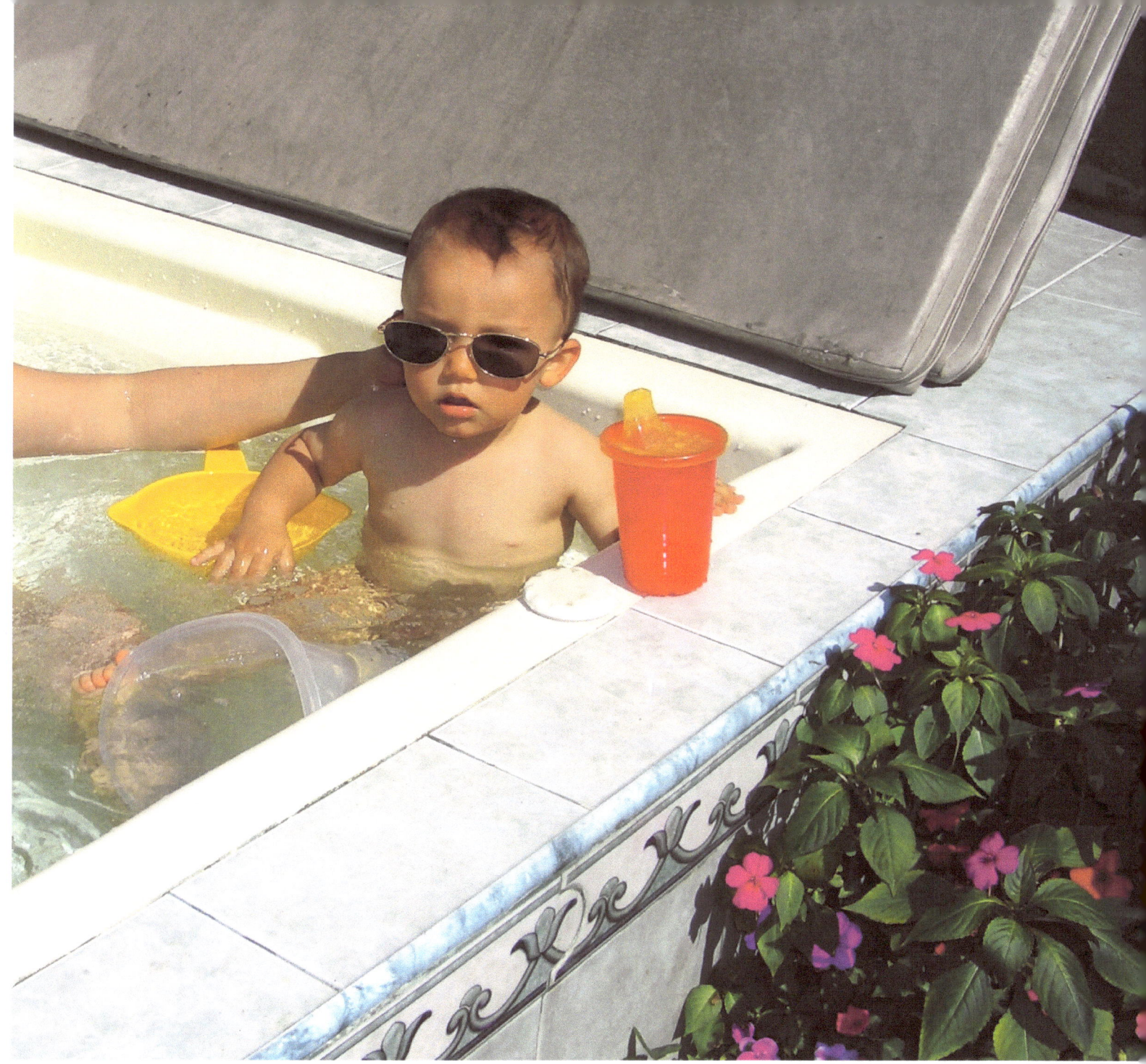

I'm not sure which is more fun . . . the bathtub or the hot tub.

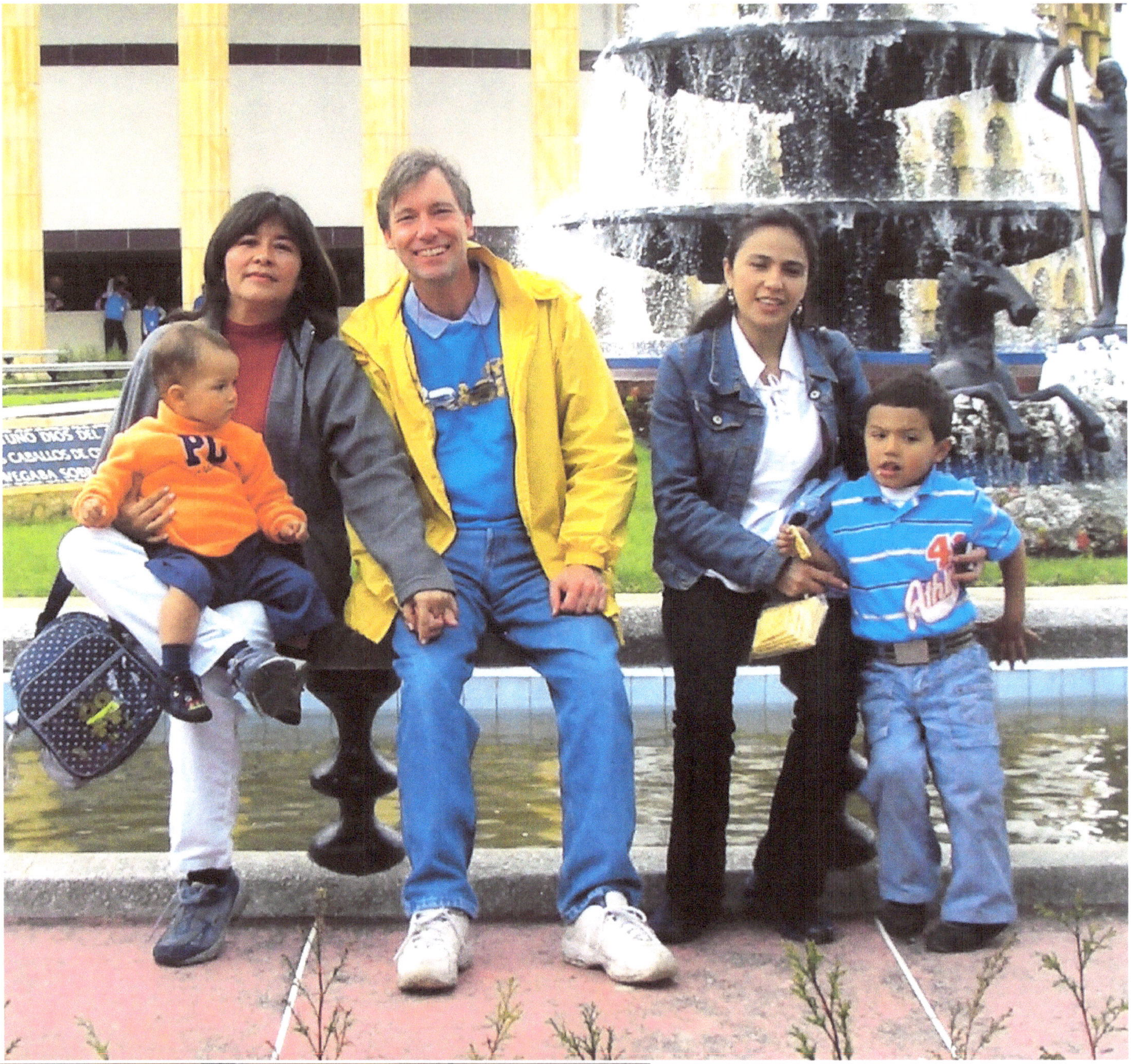

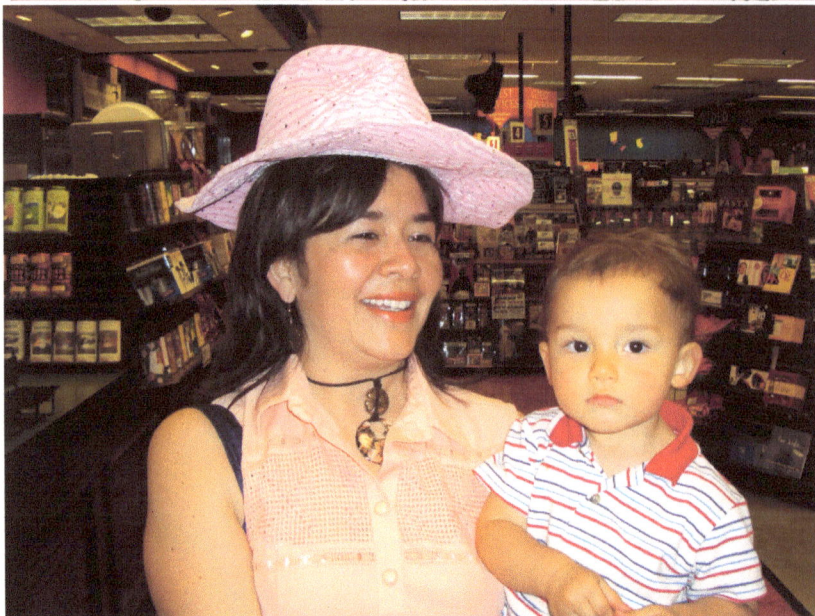

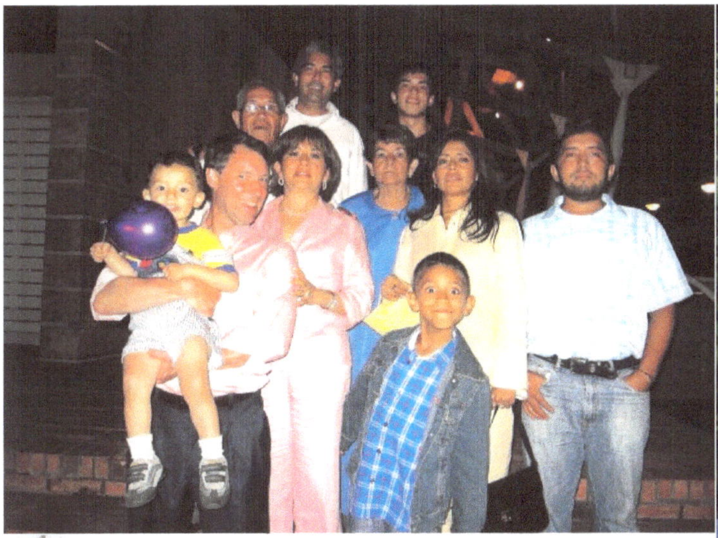

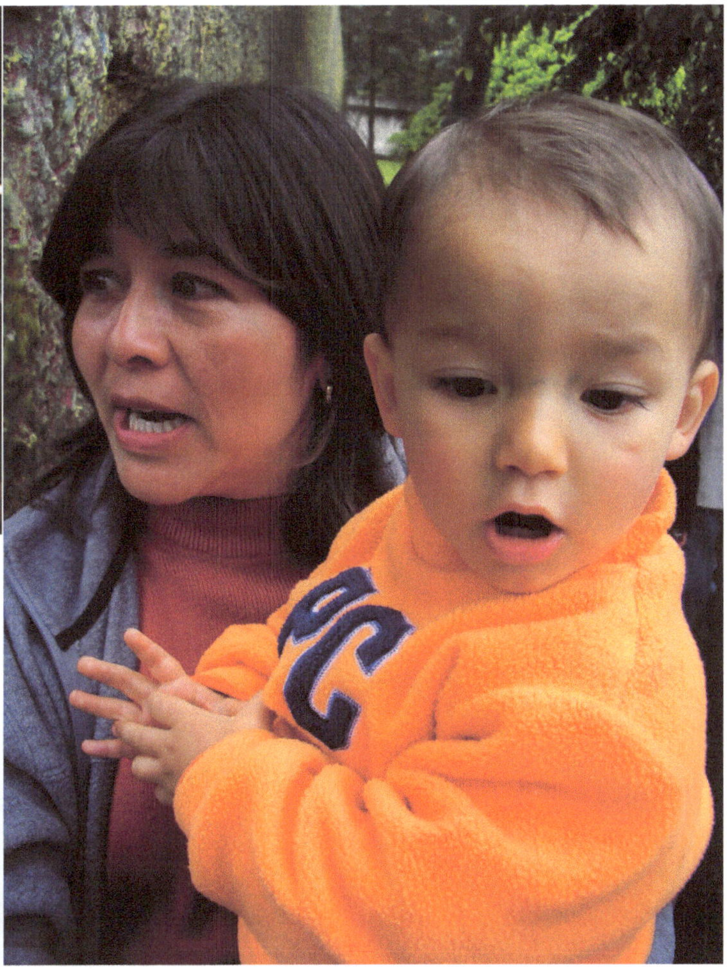

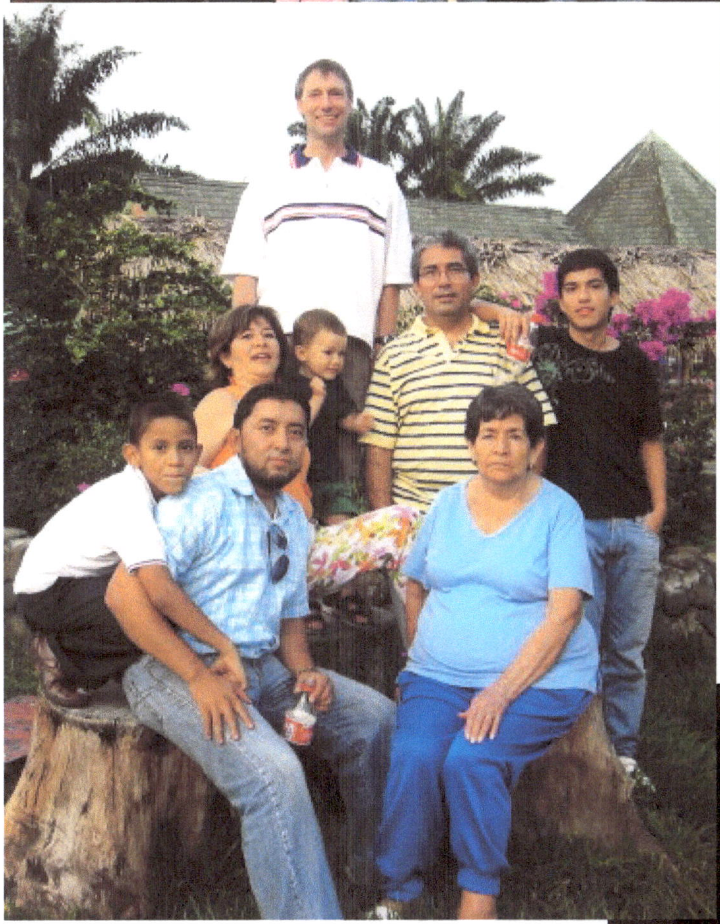

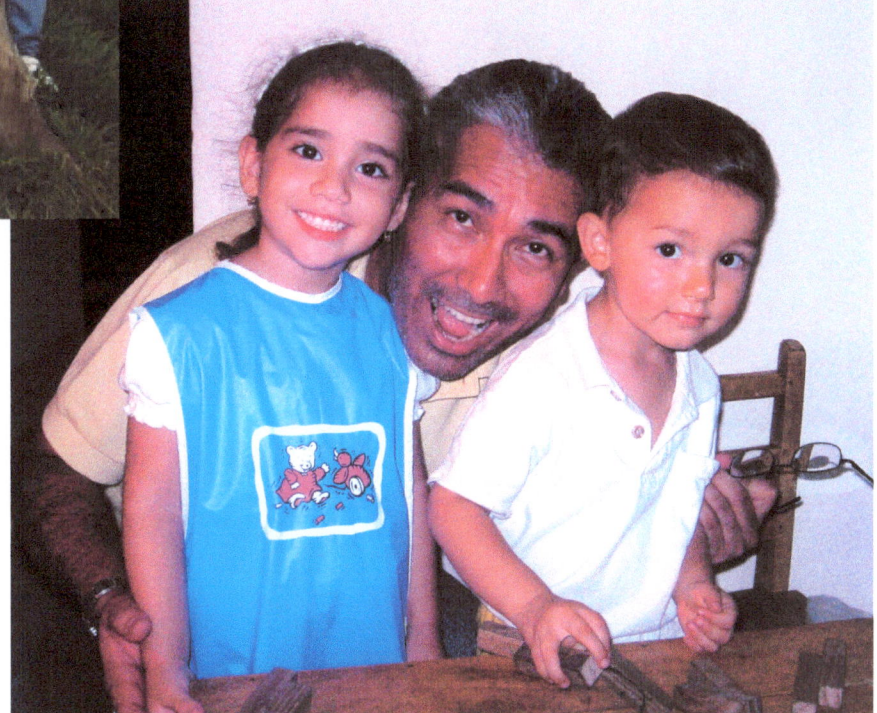

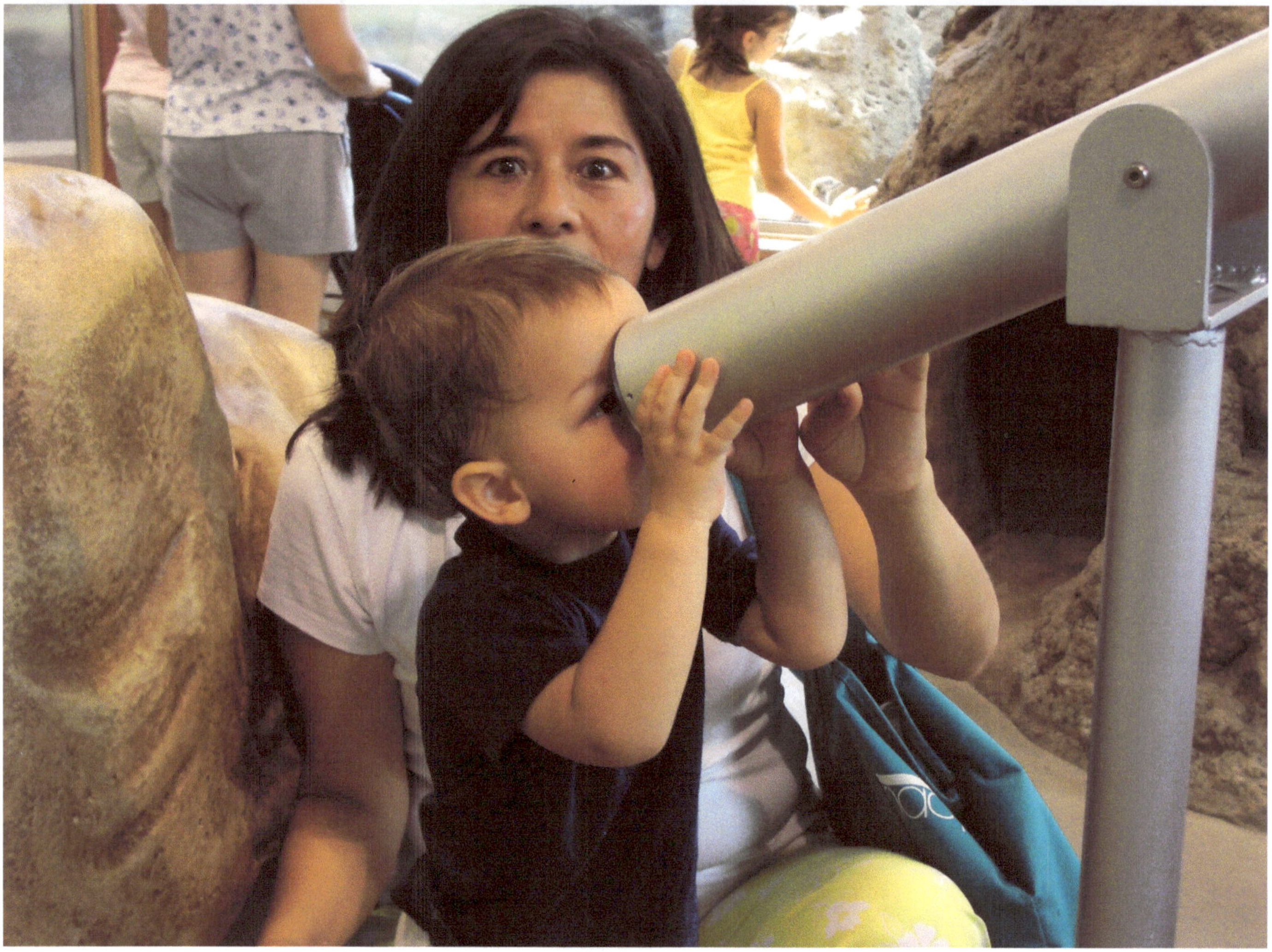

Curiosity is my middle name.

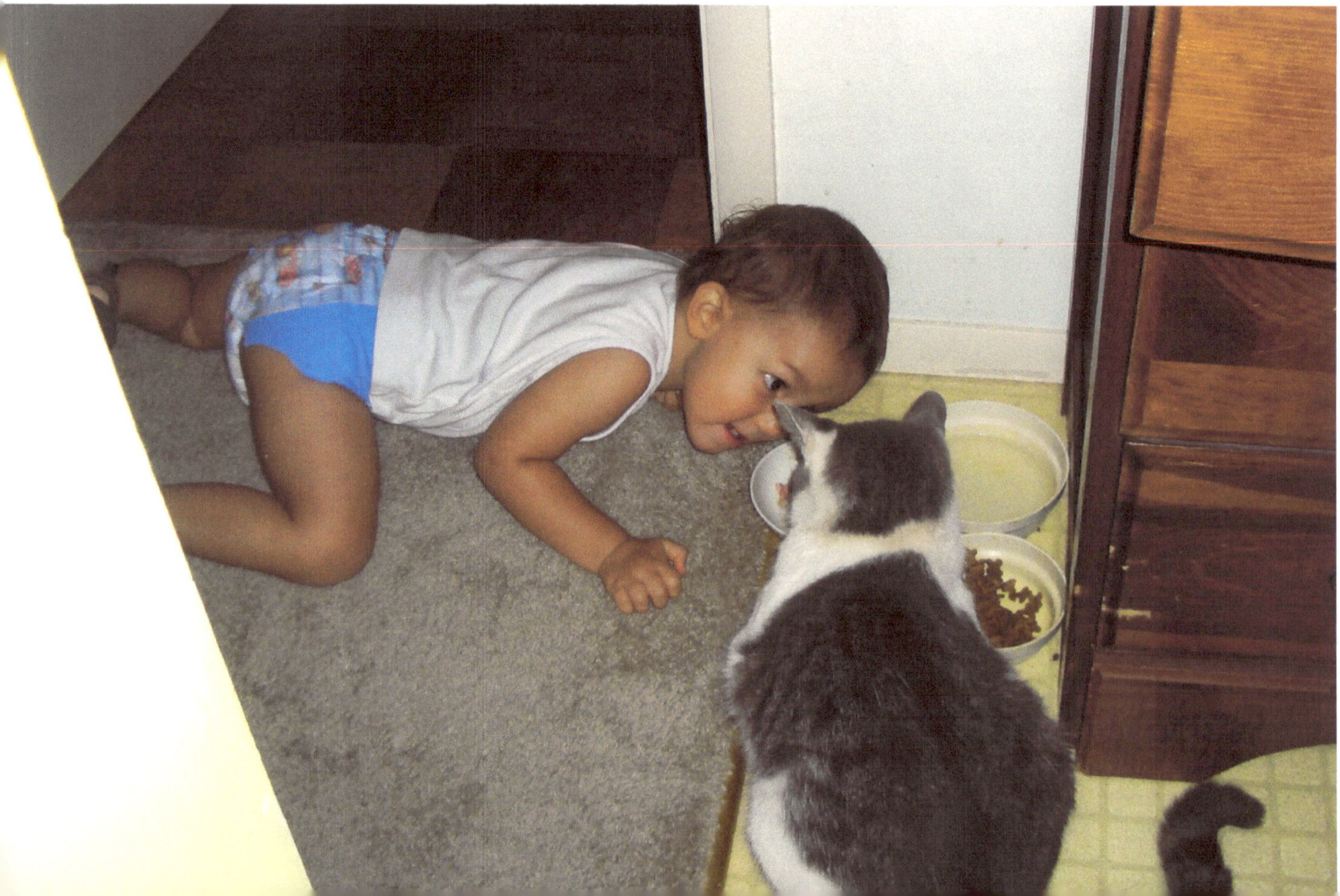

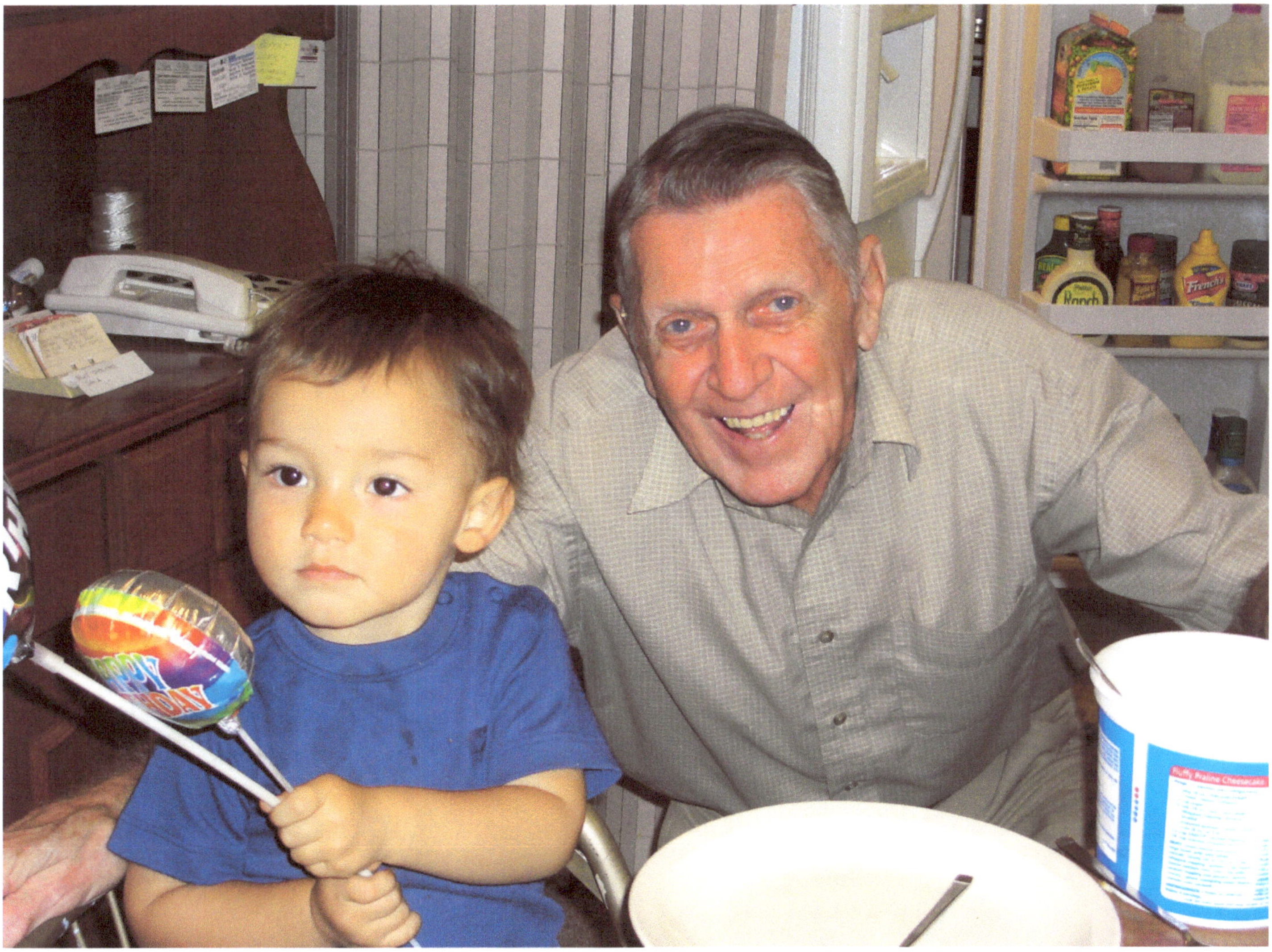

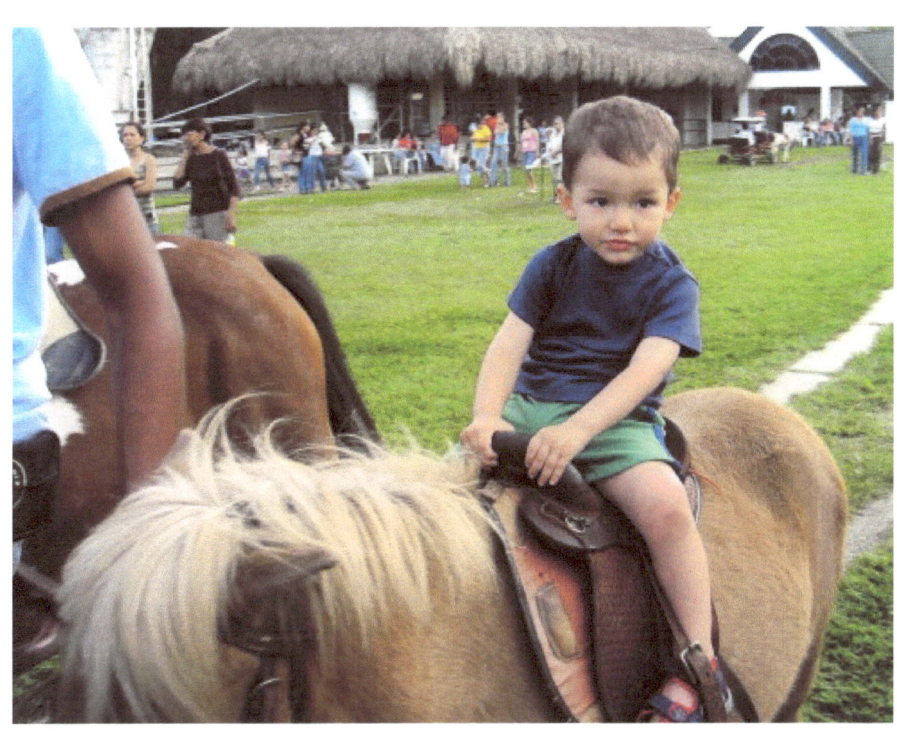

I love Grandpa Jim, but I'm not so sure about riding ponies.

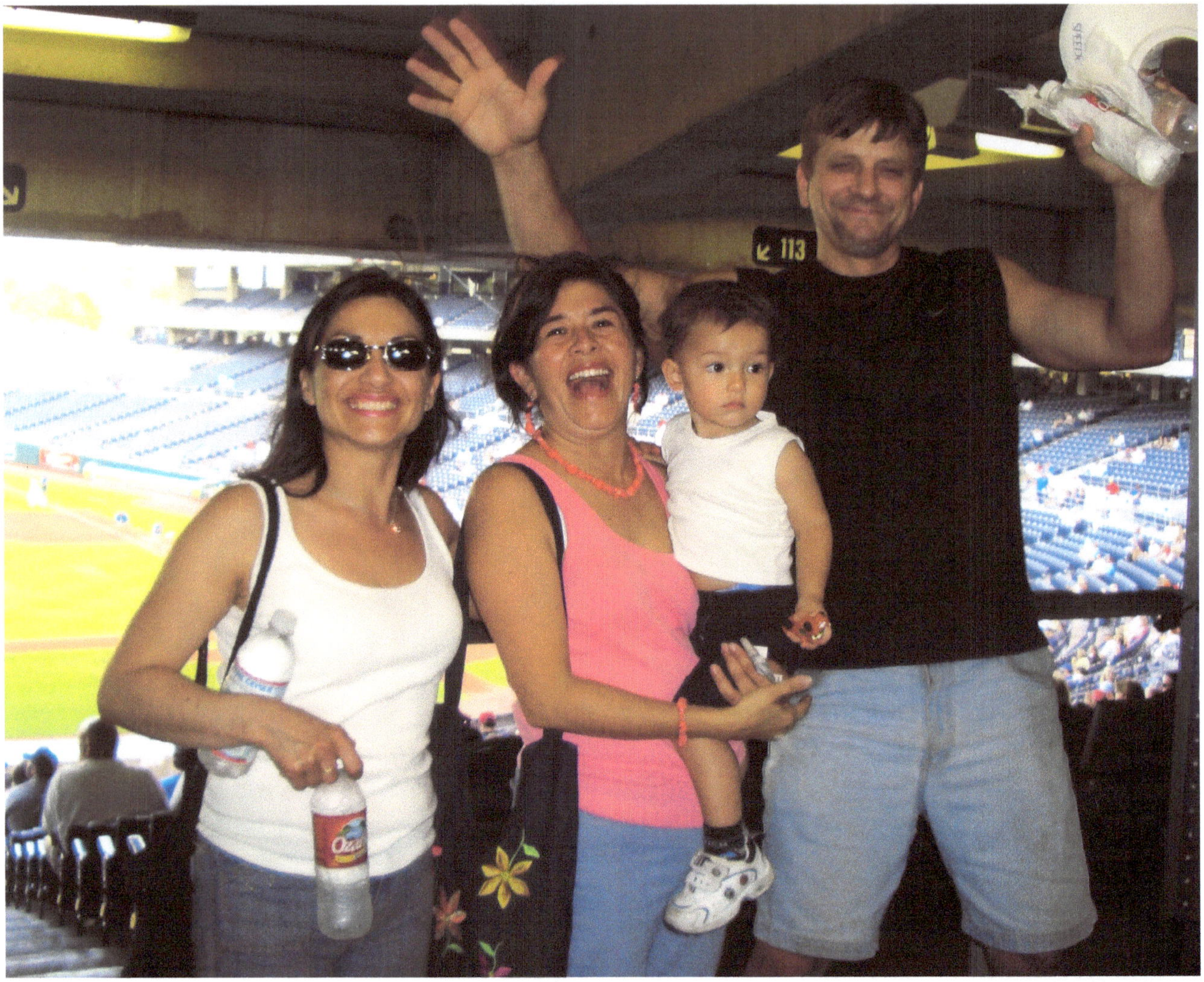
113

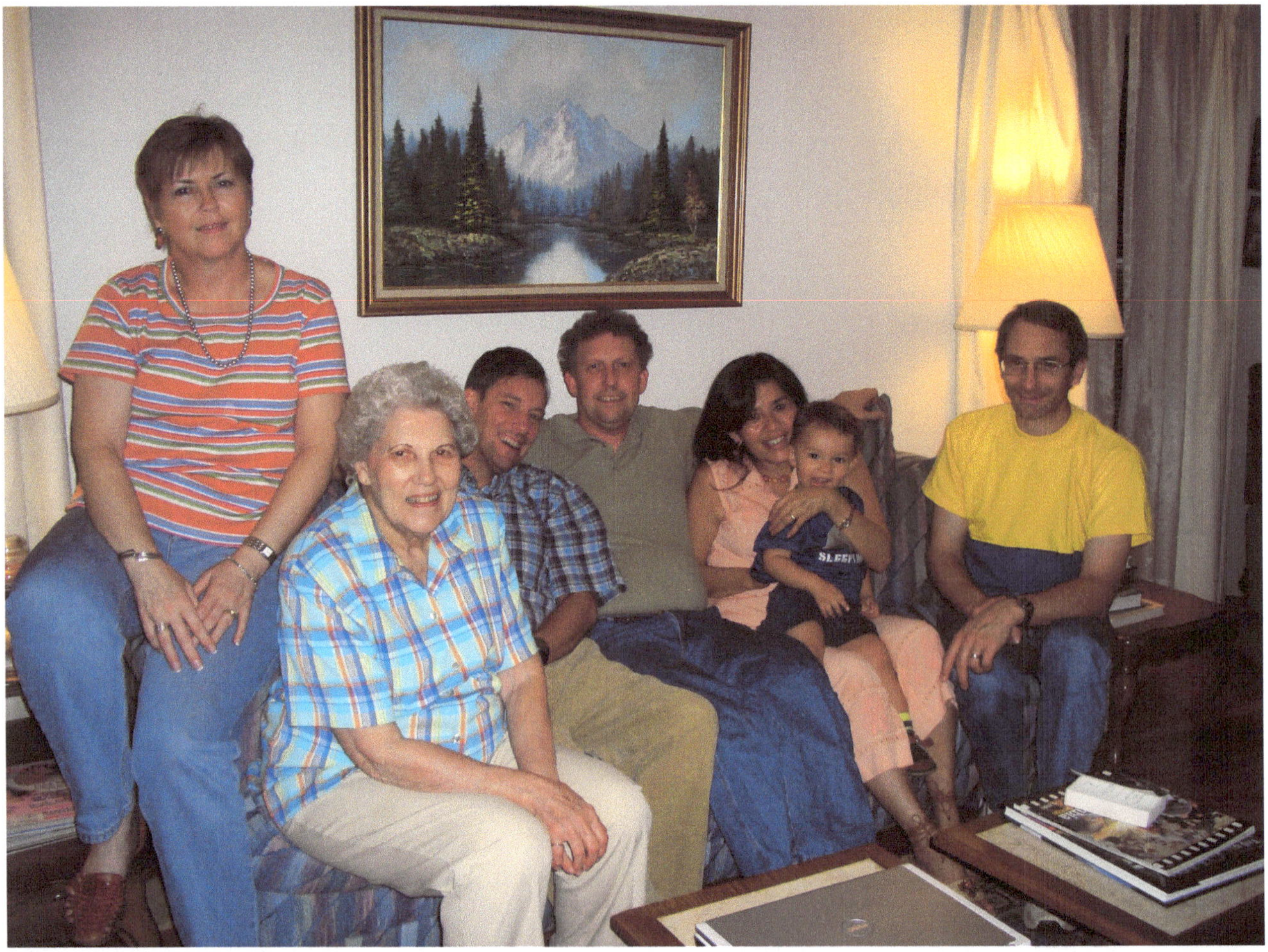

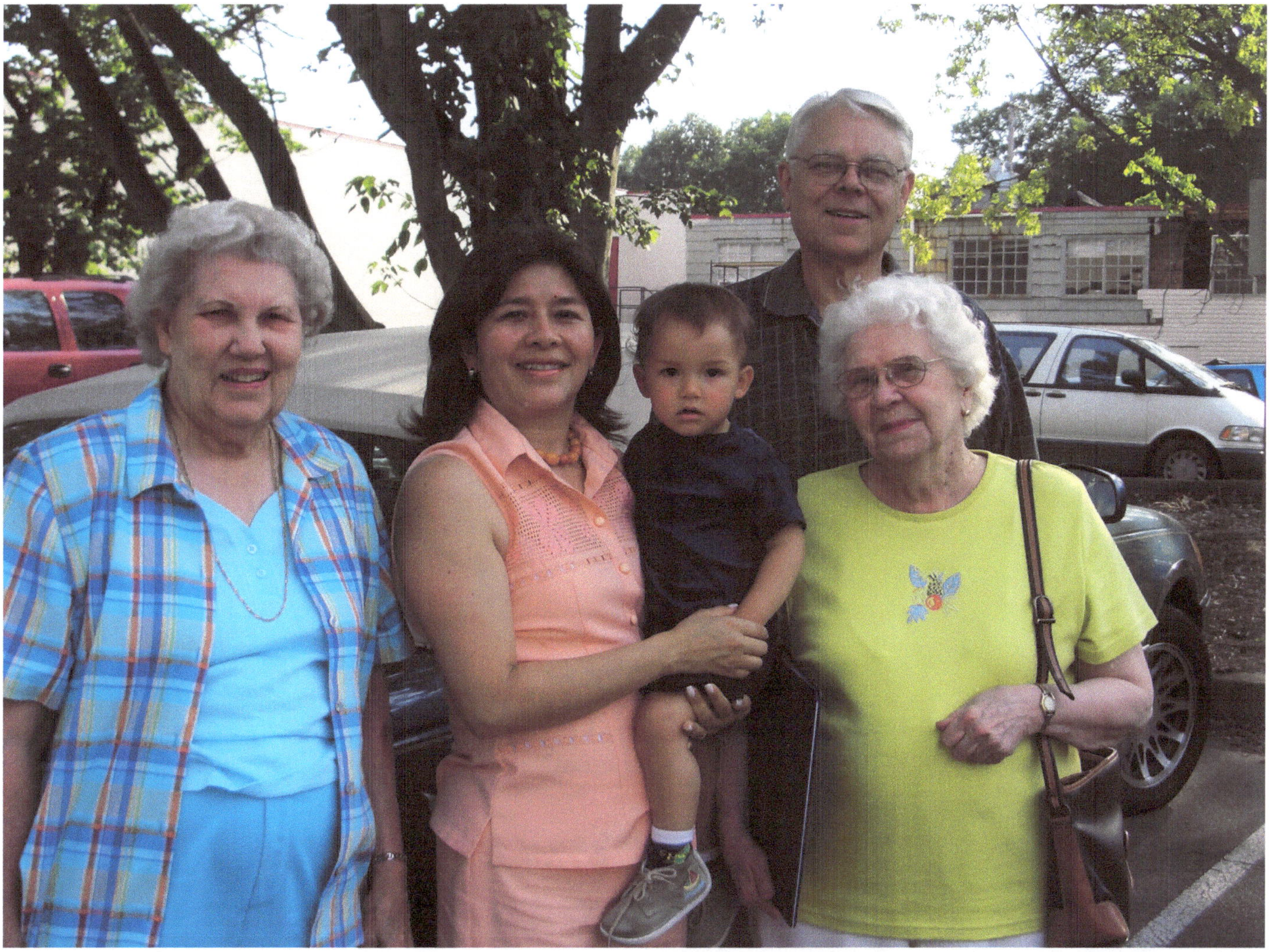

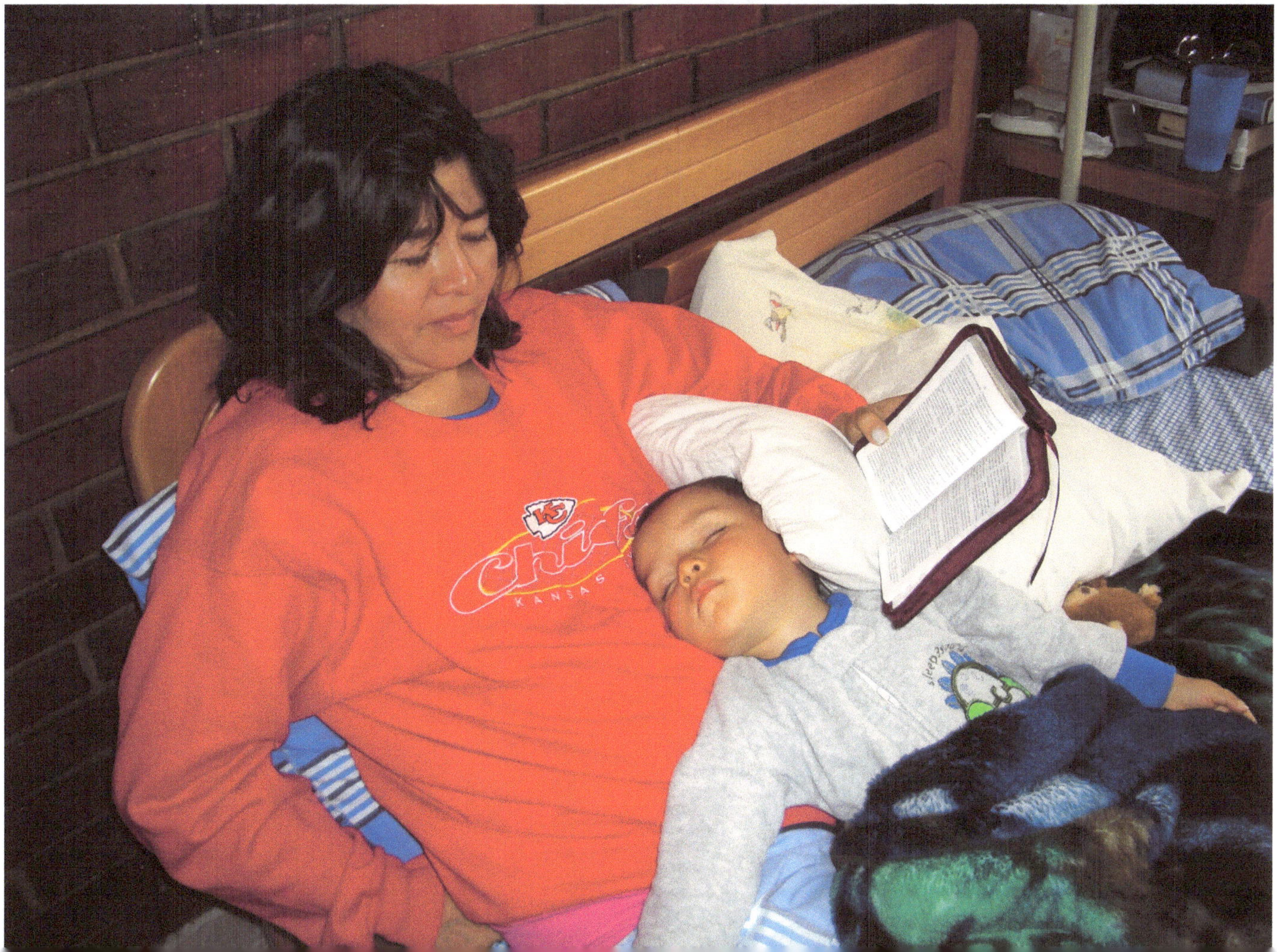
KANSAS

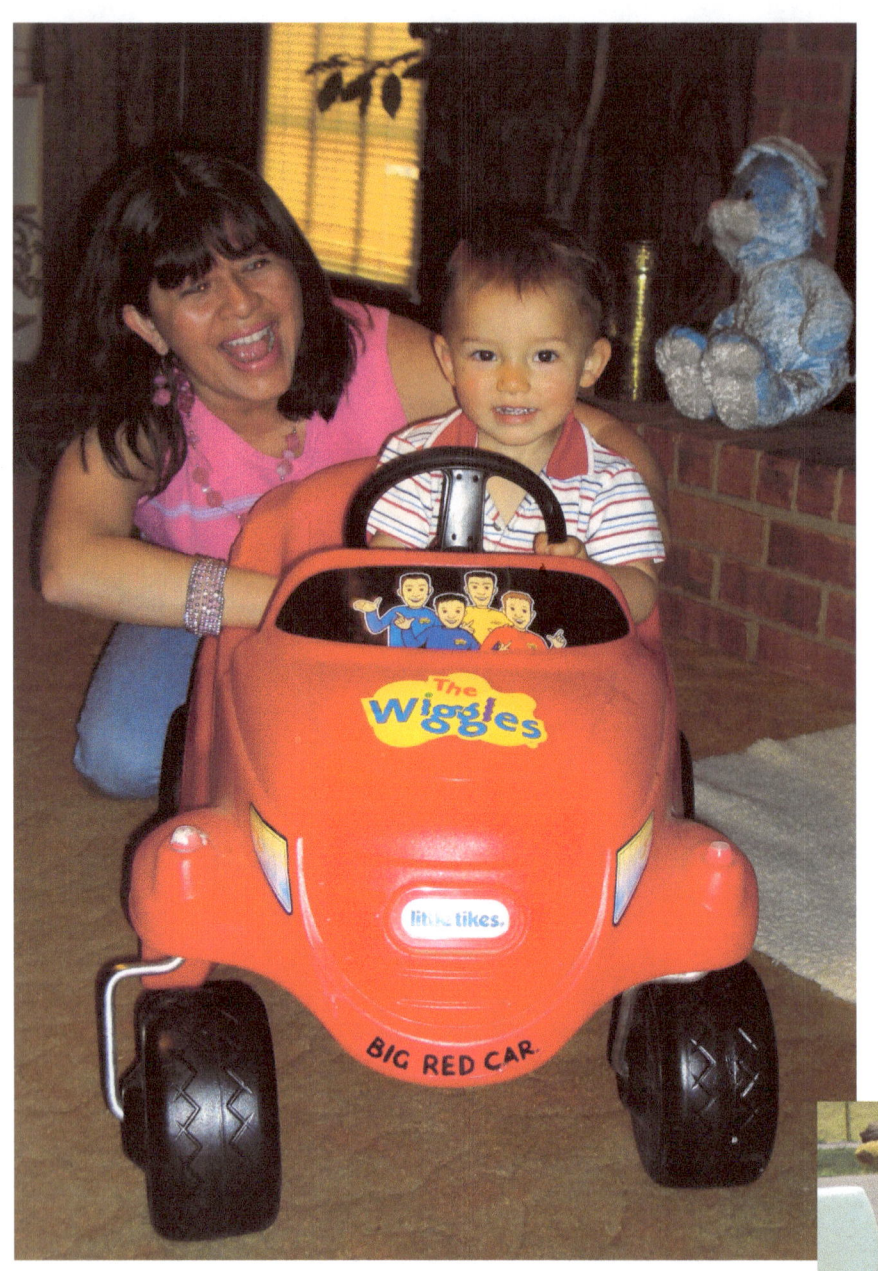

Is this a real dinasour,
Mama?

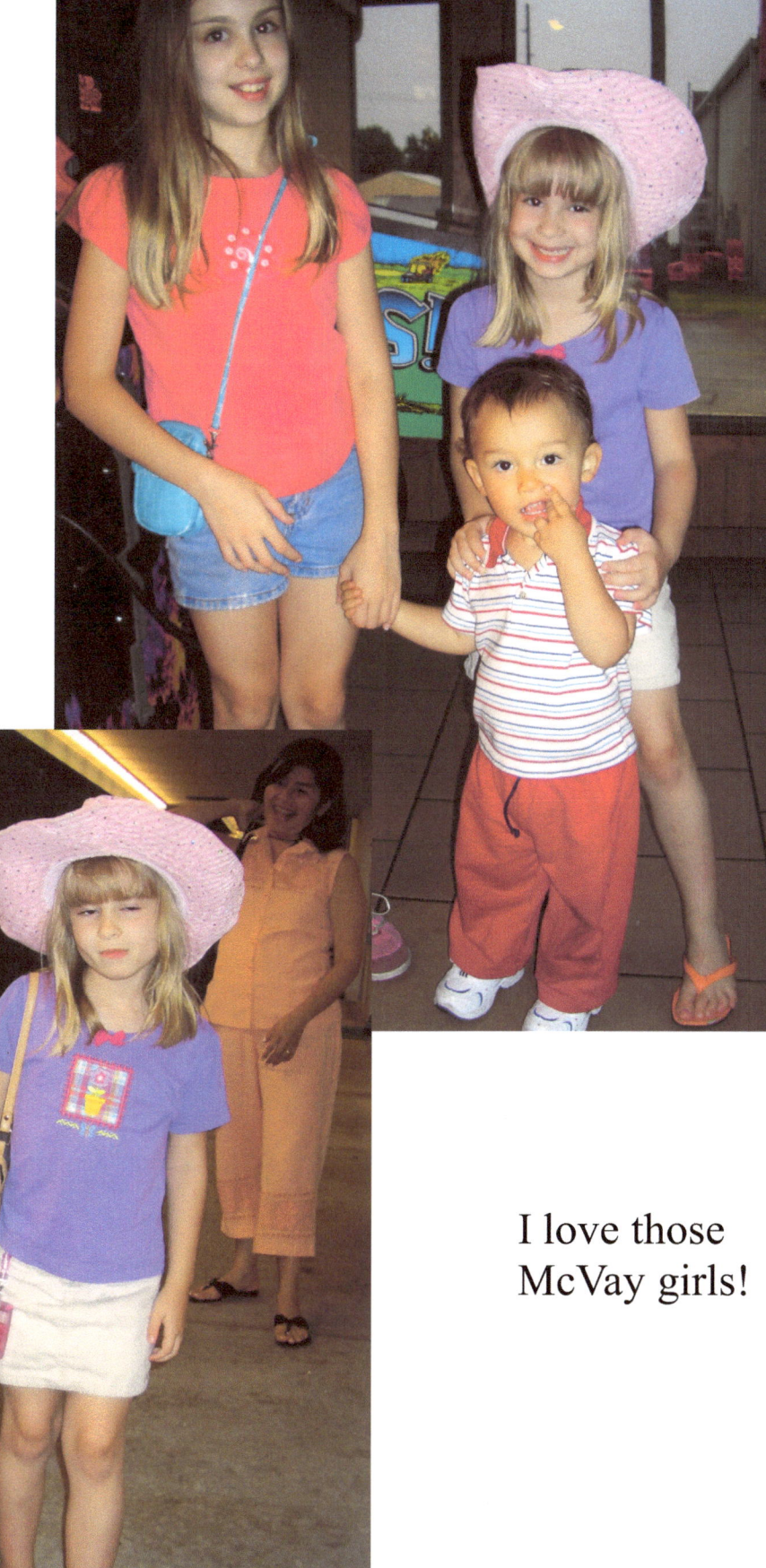

I love those
McVay girls!

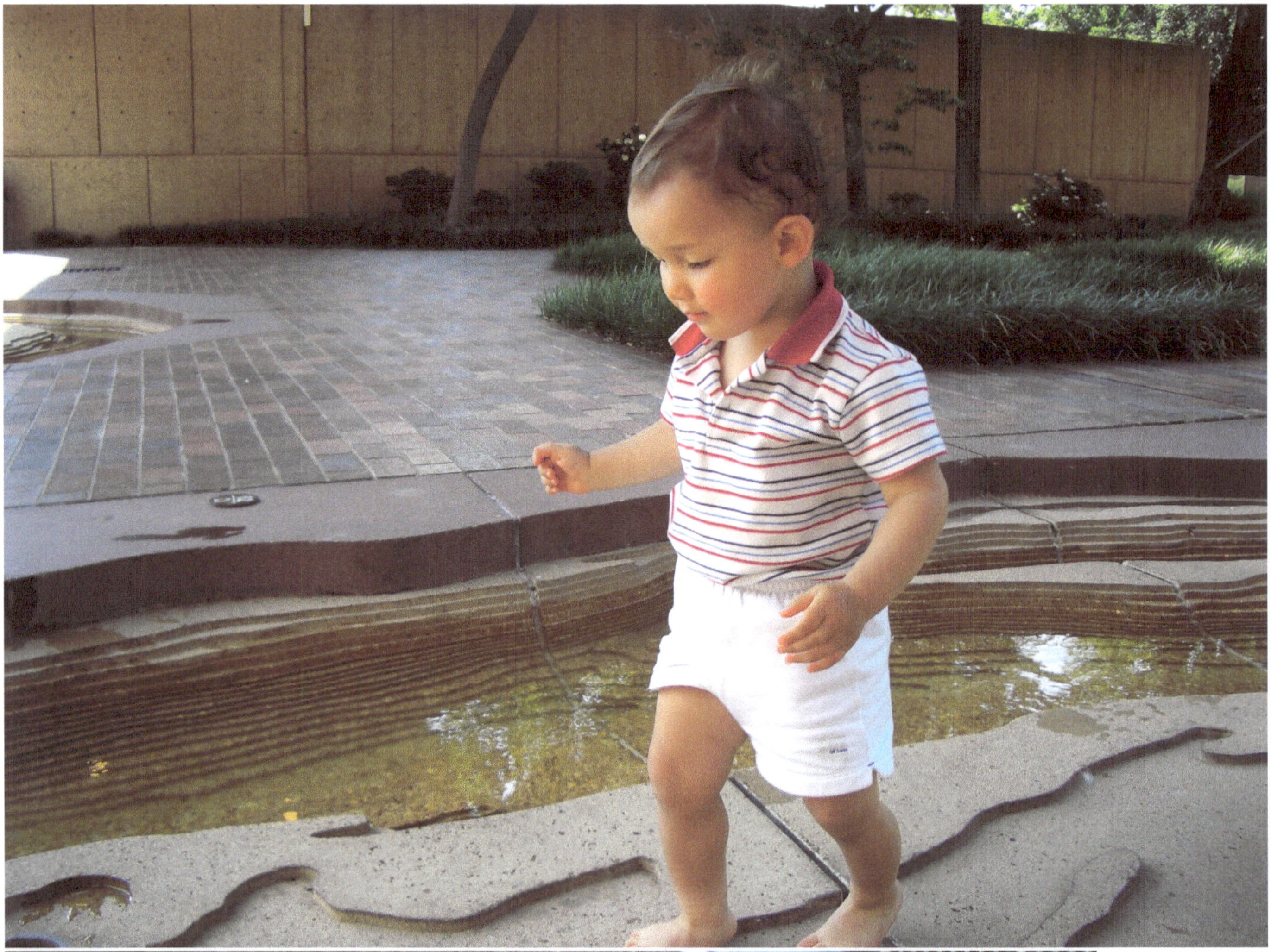

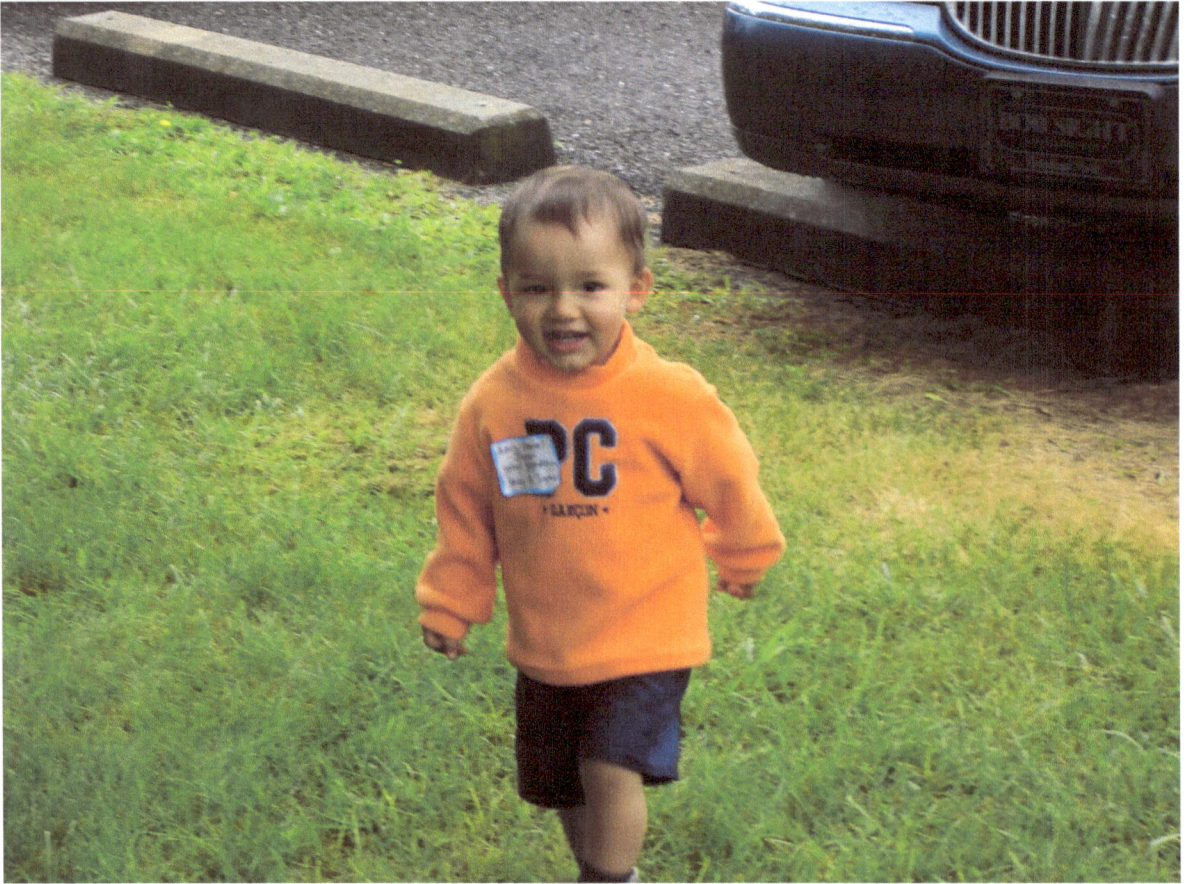

Right: The
Soper
reunion.

Left: Walk-
ing the
Mississippi

Below: Red
Rocks, CO

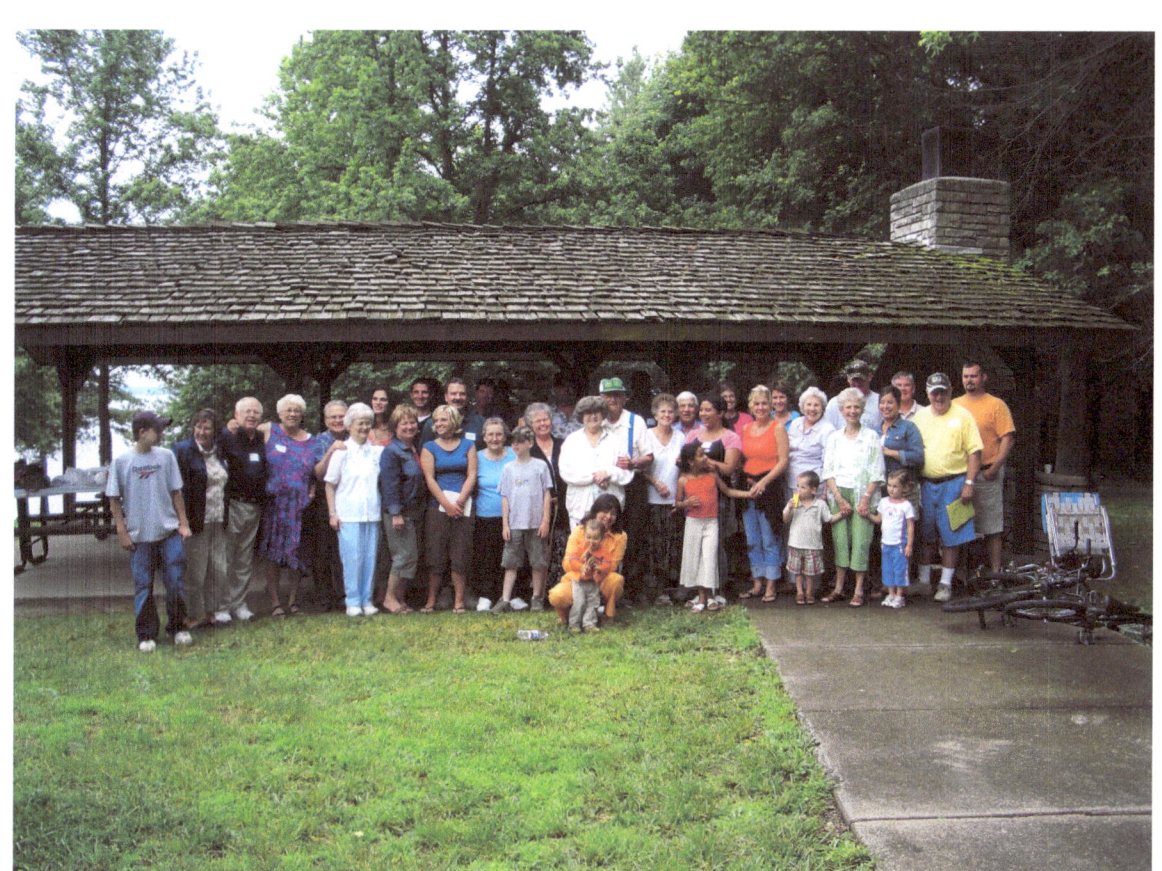

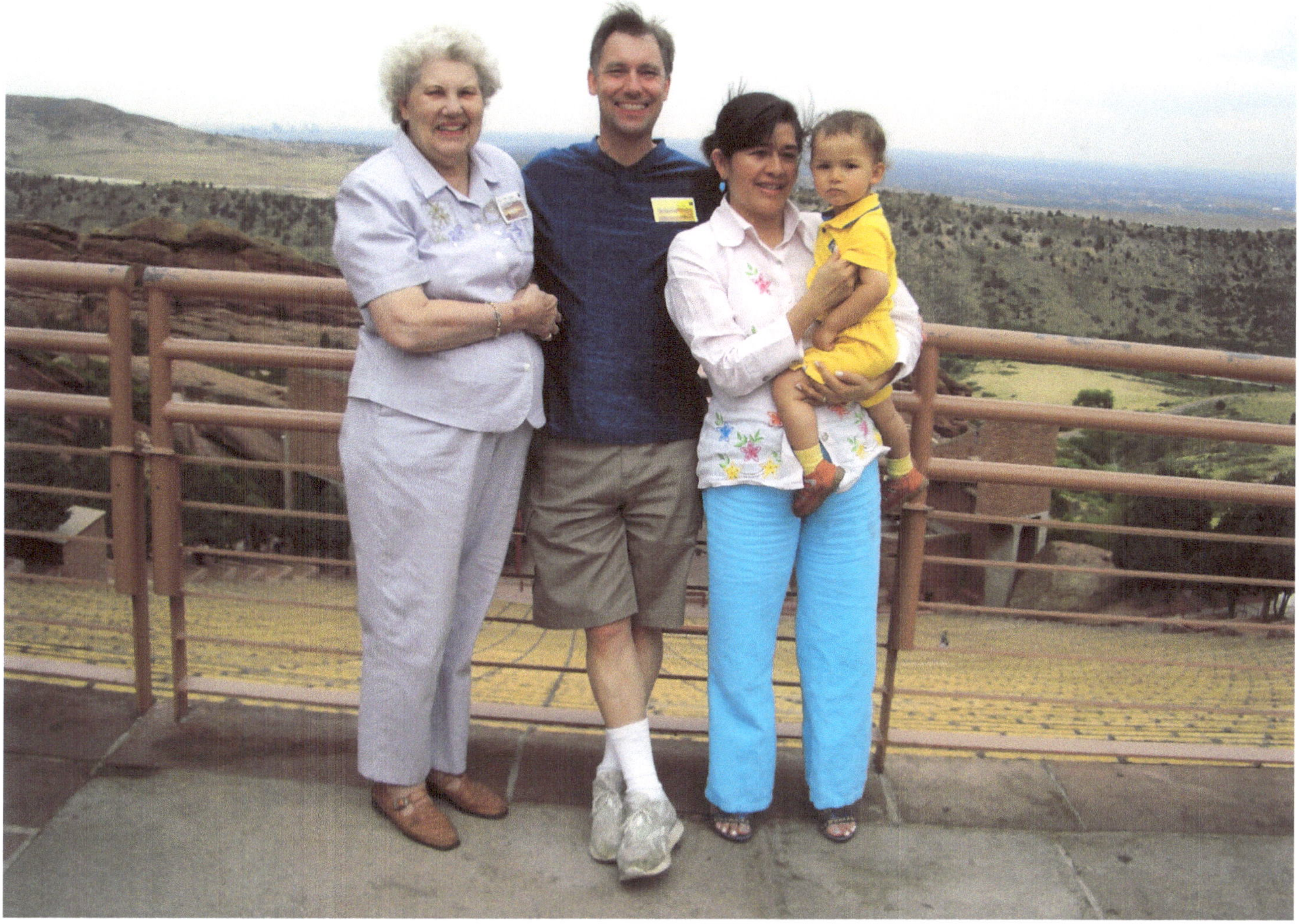

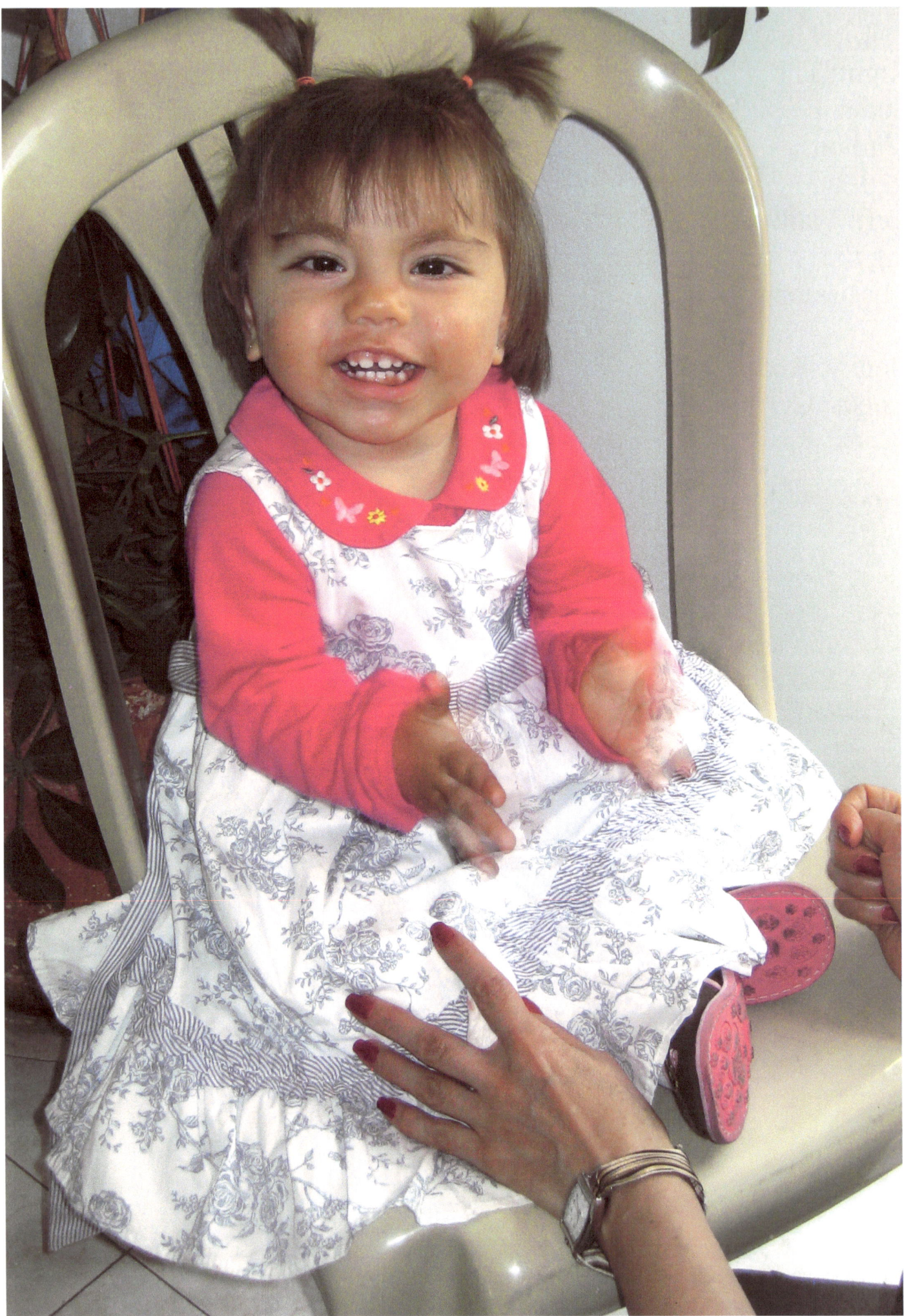

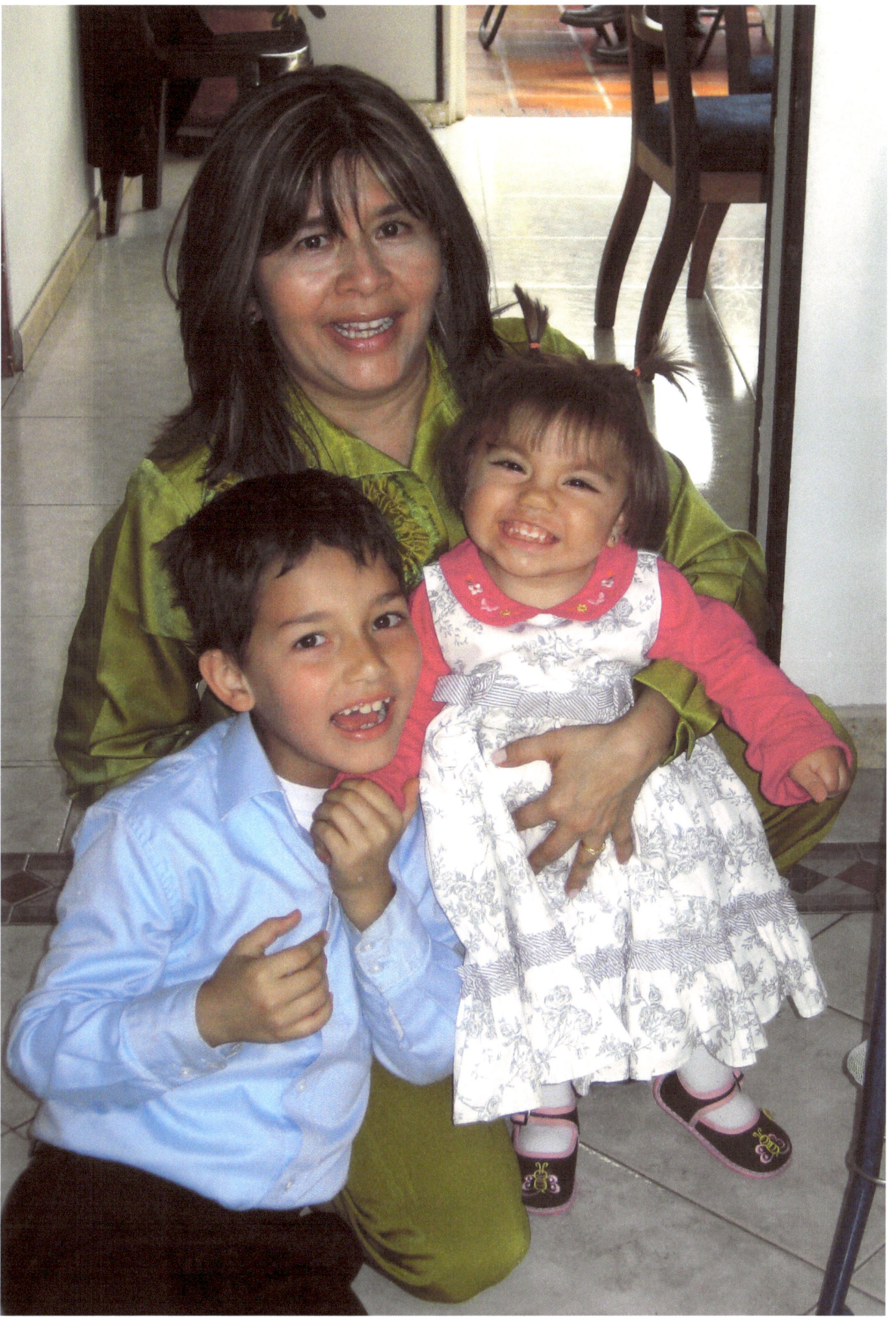

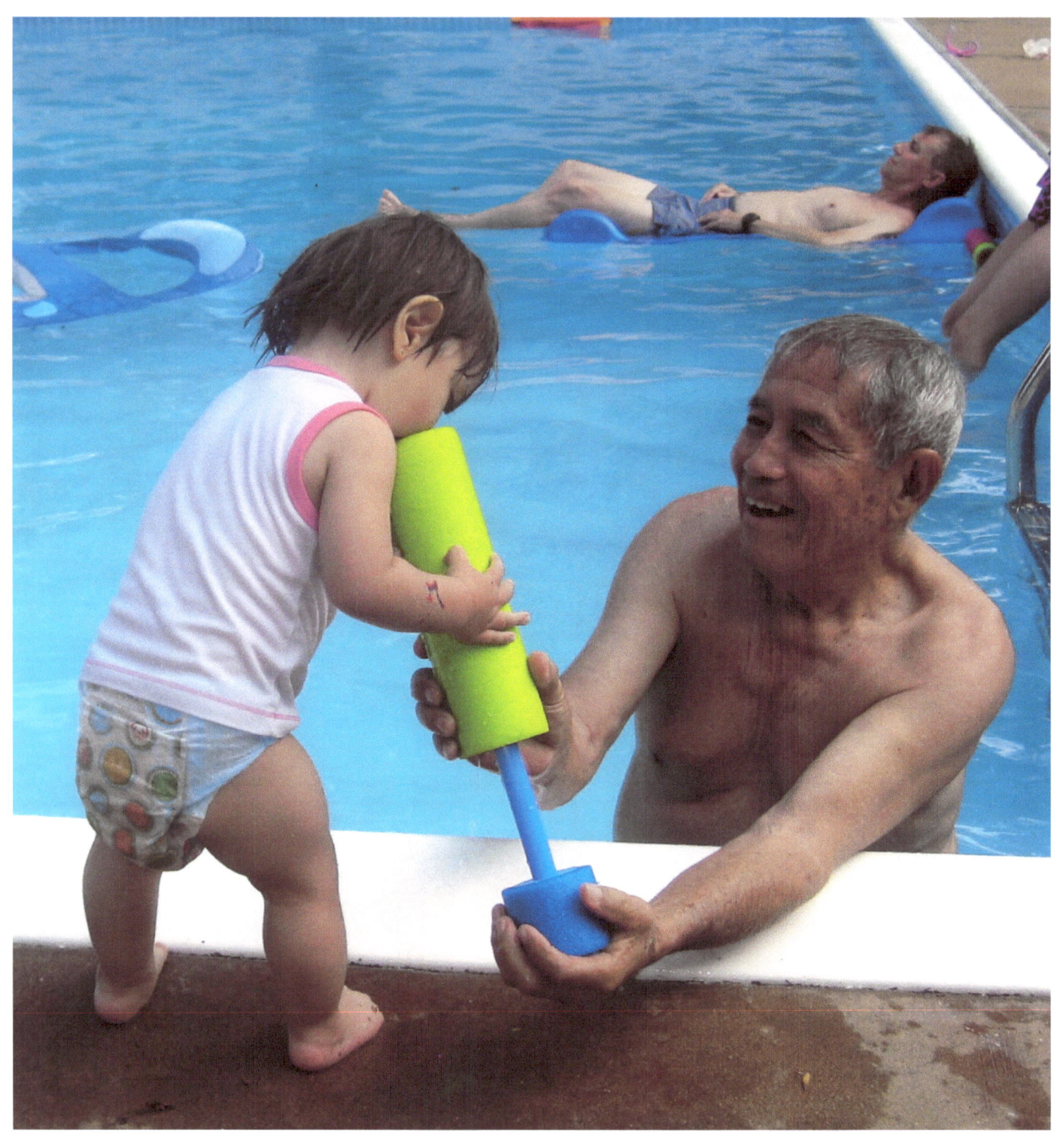

What is this, Grandpa?

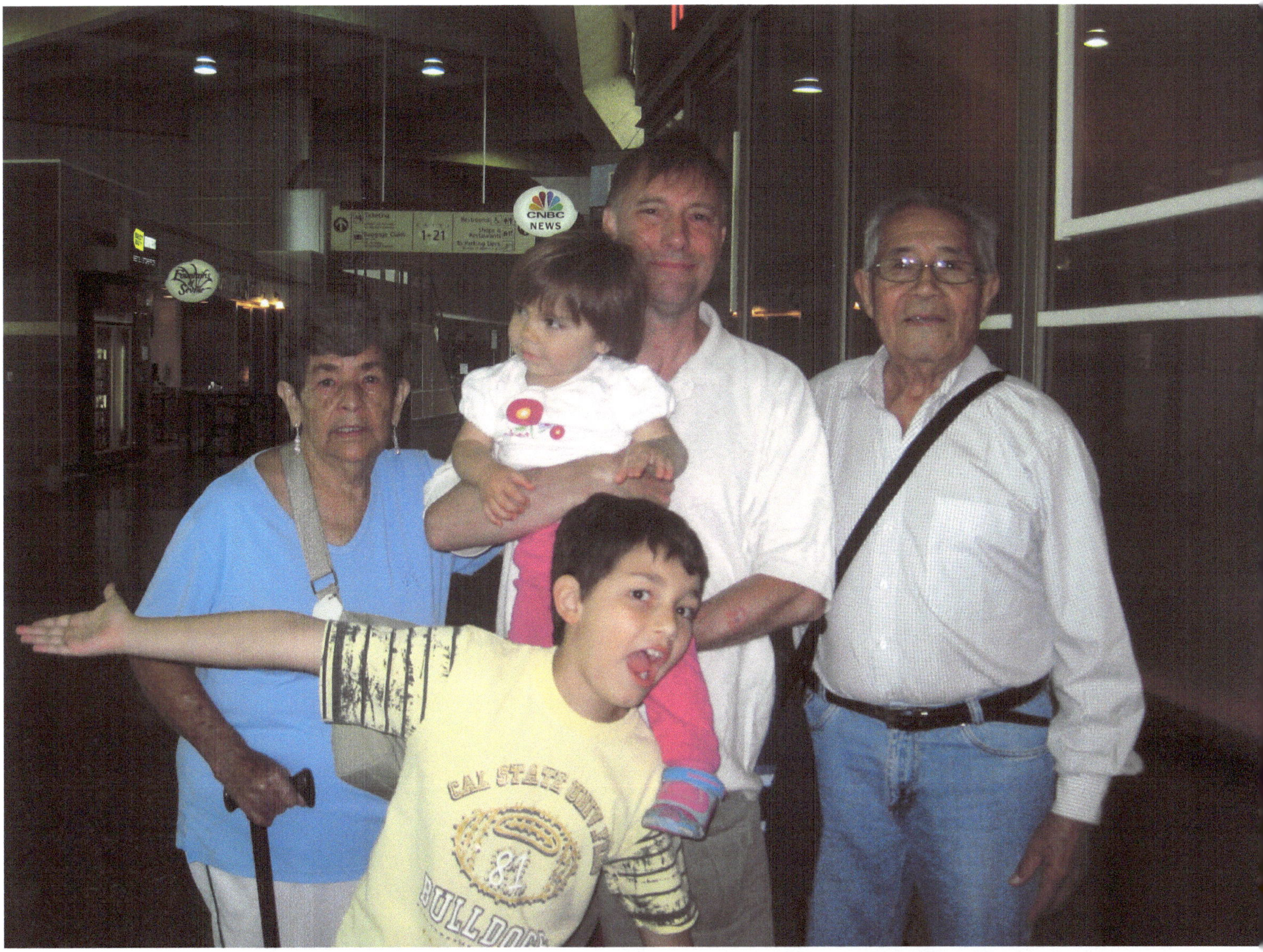

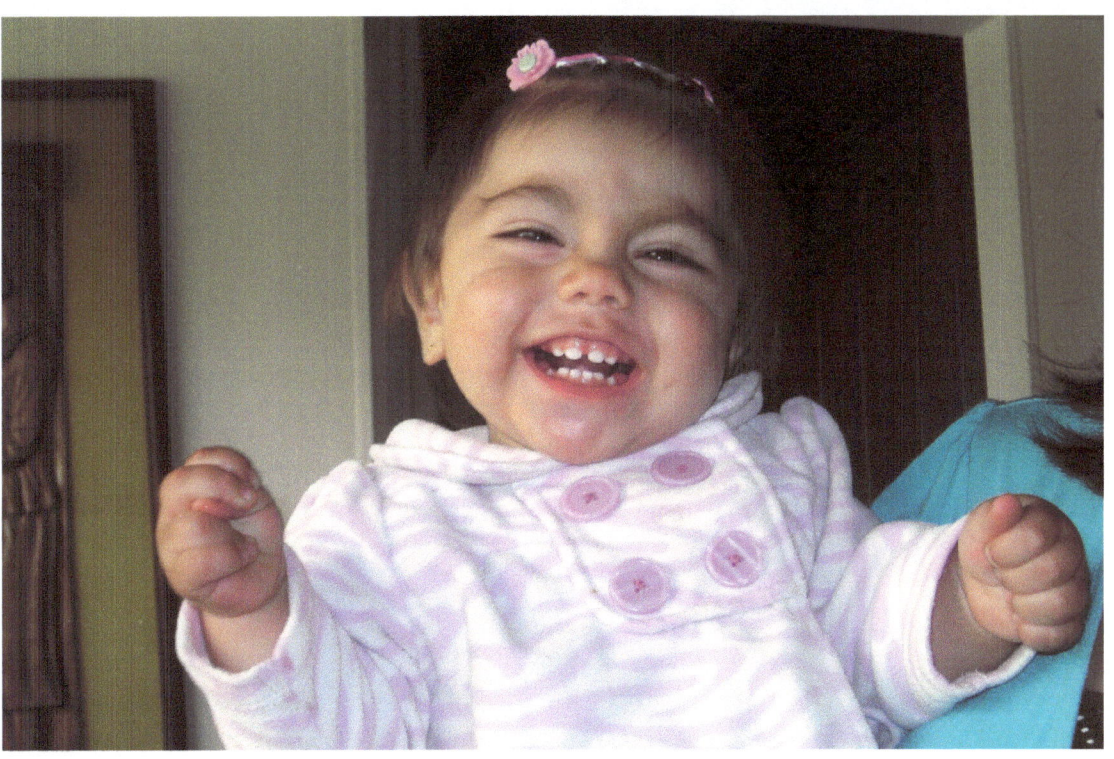

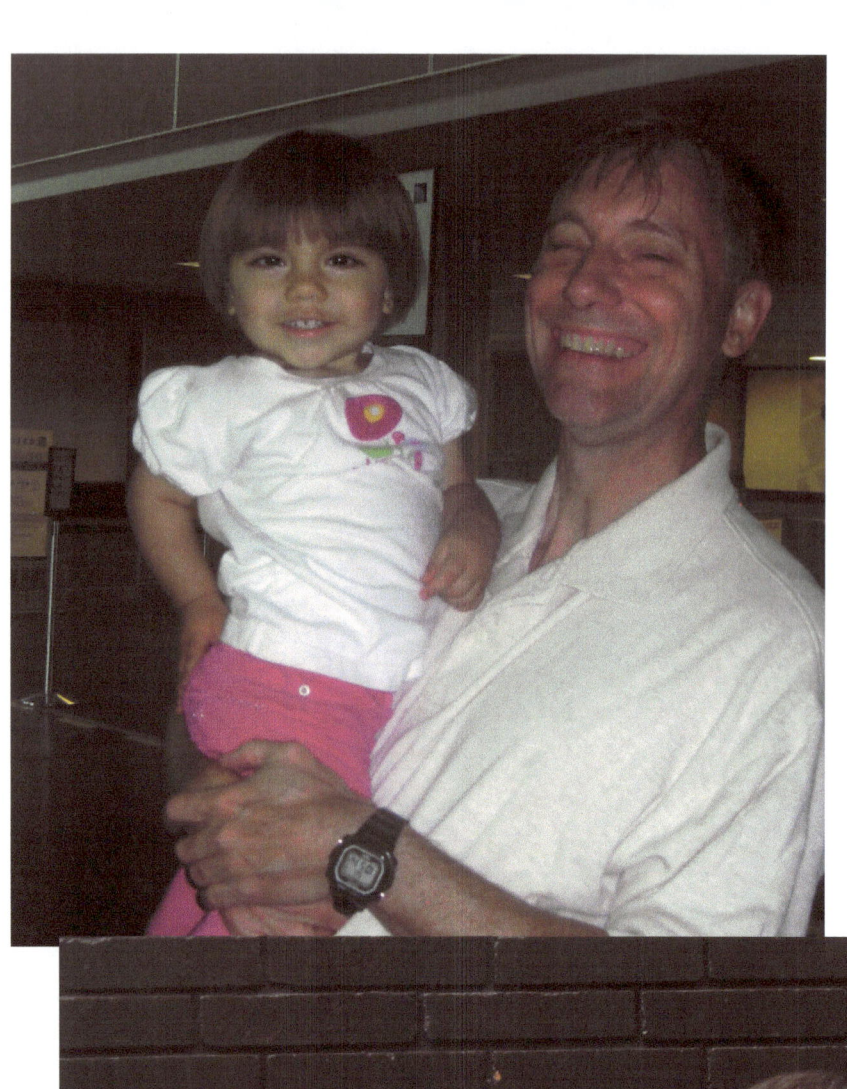

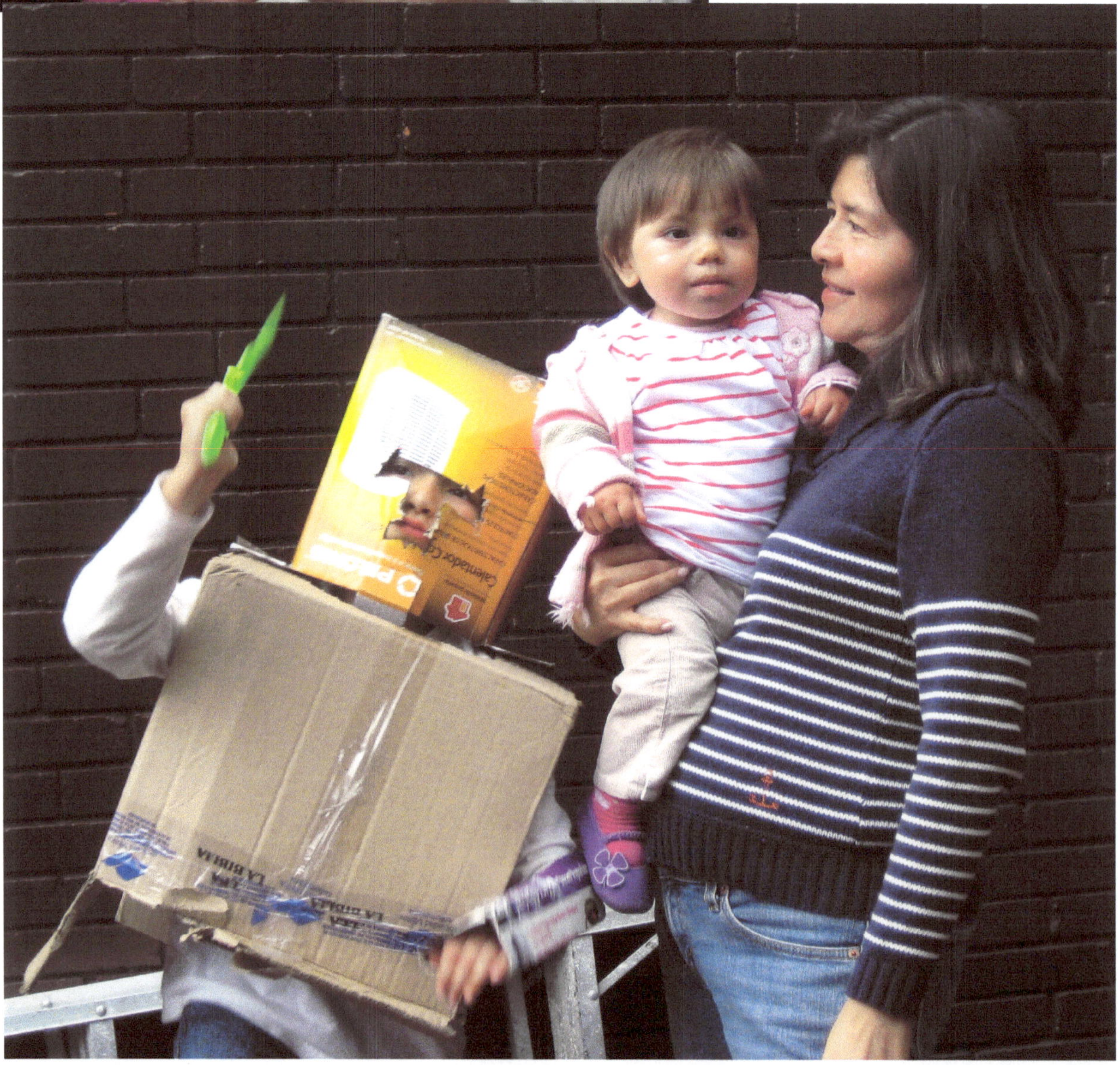

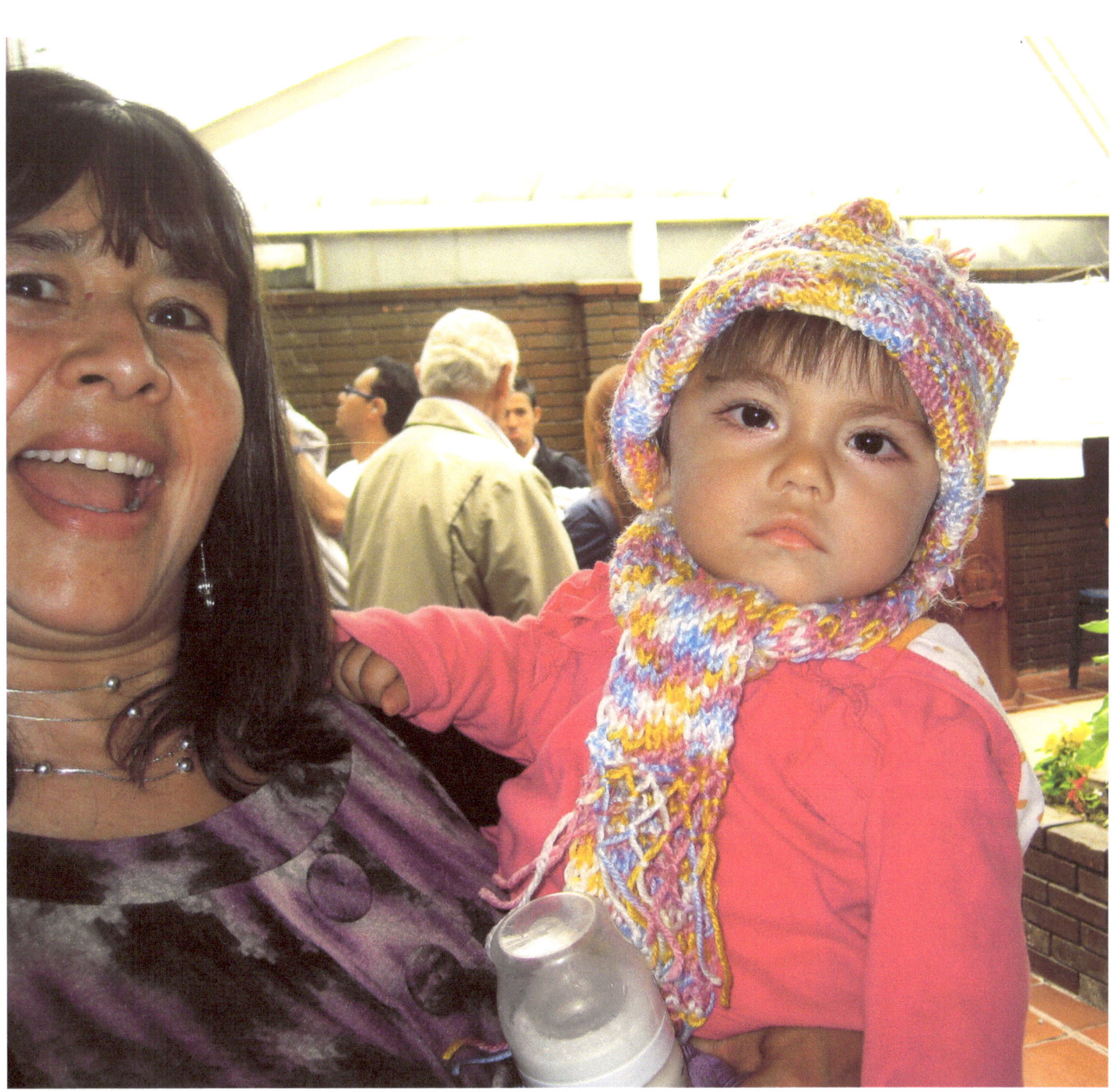

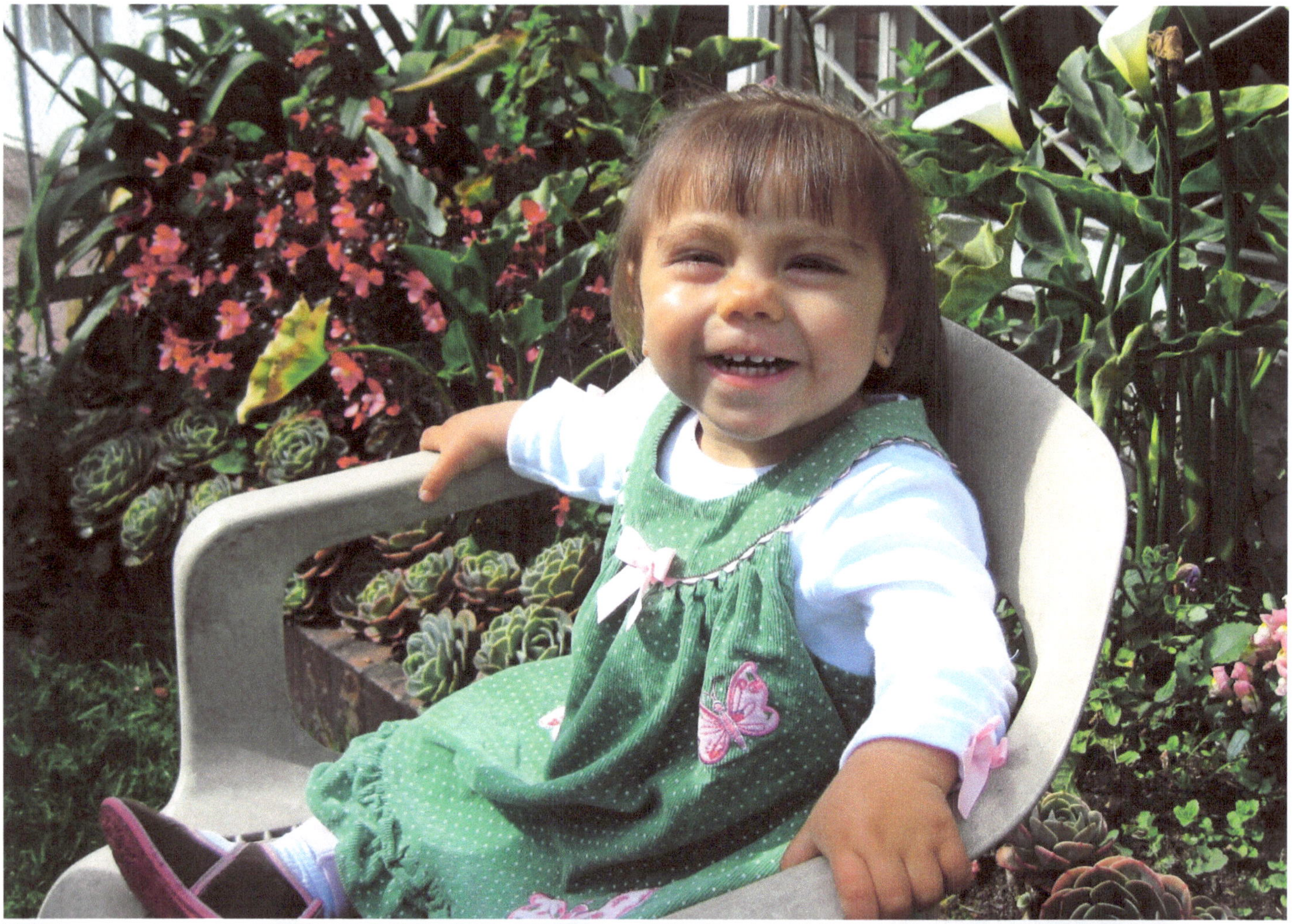

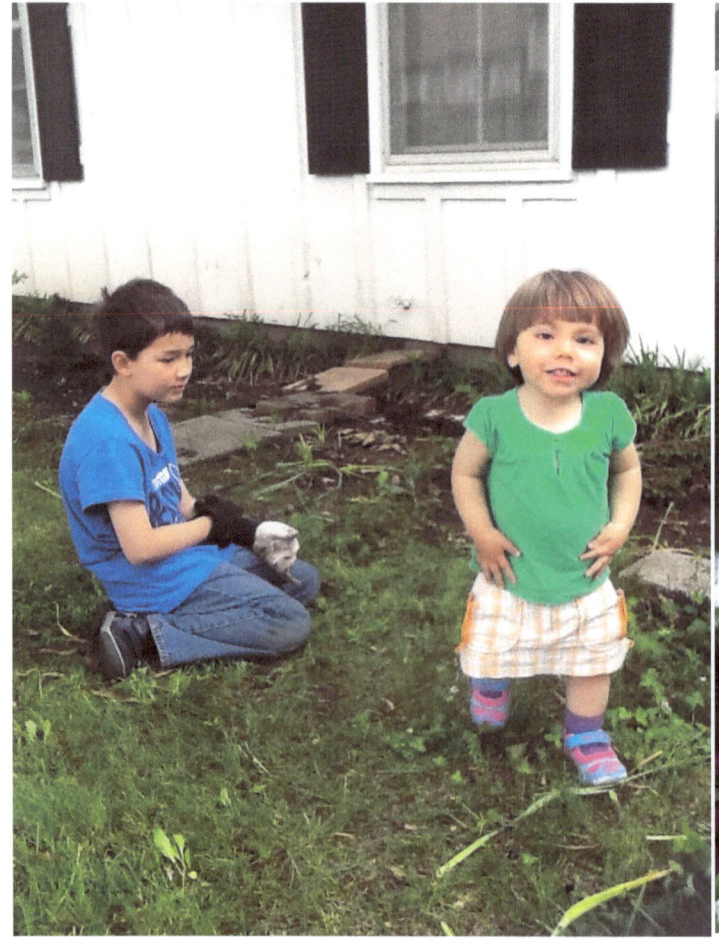
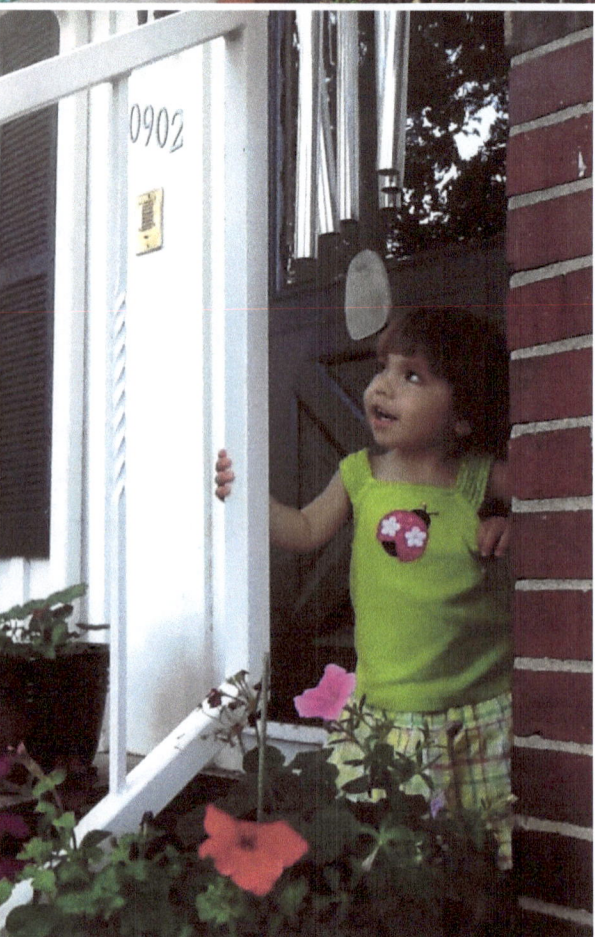

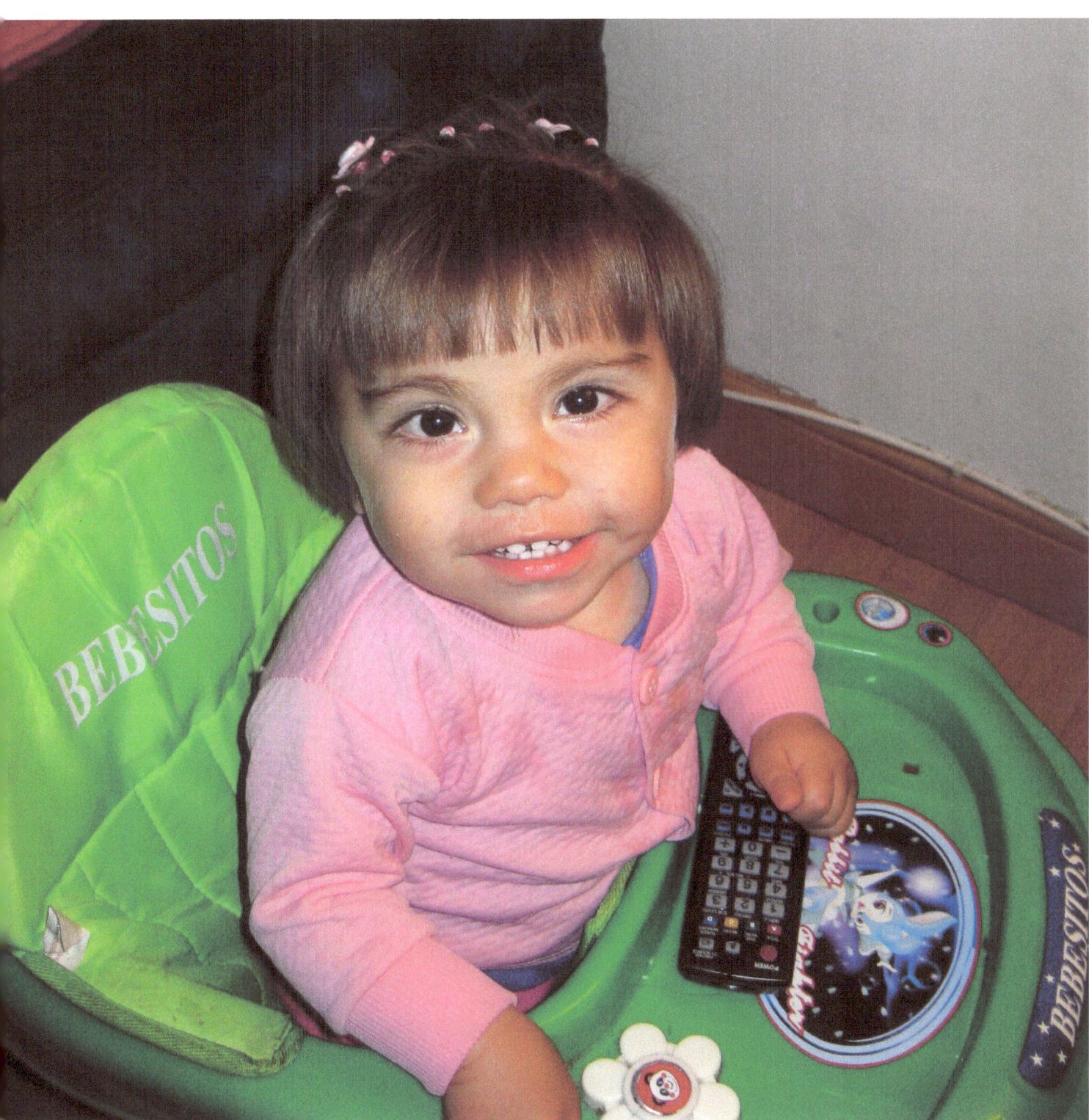

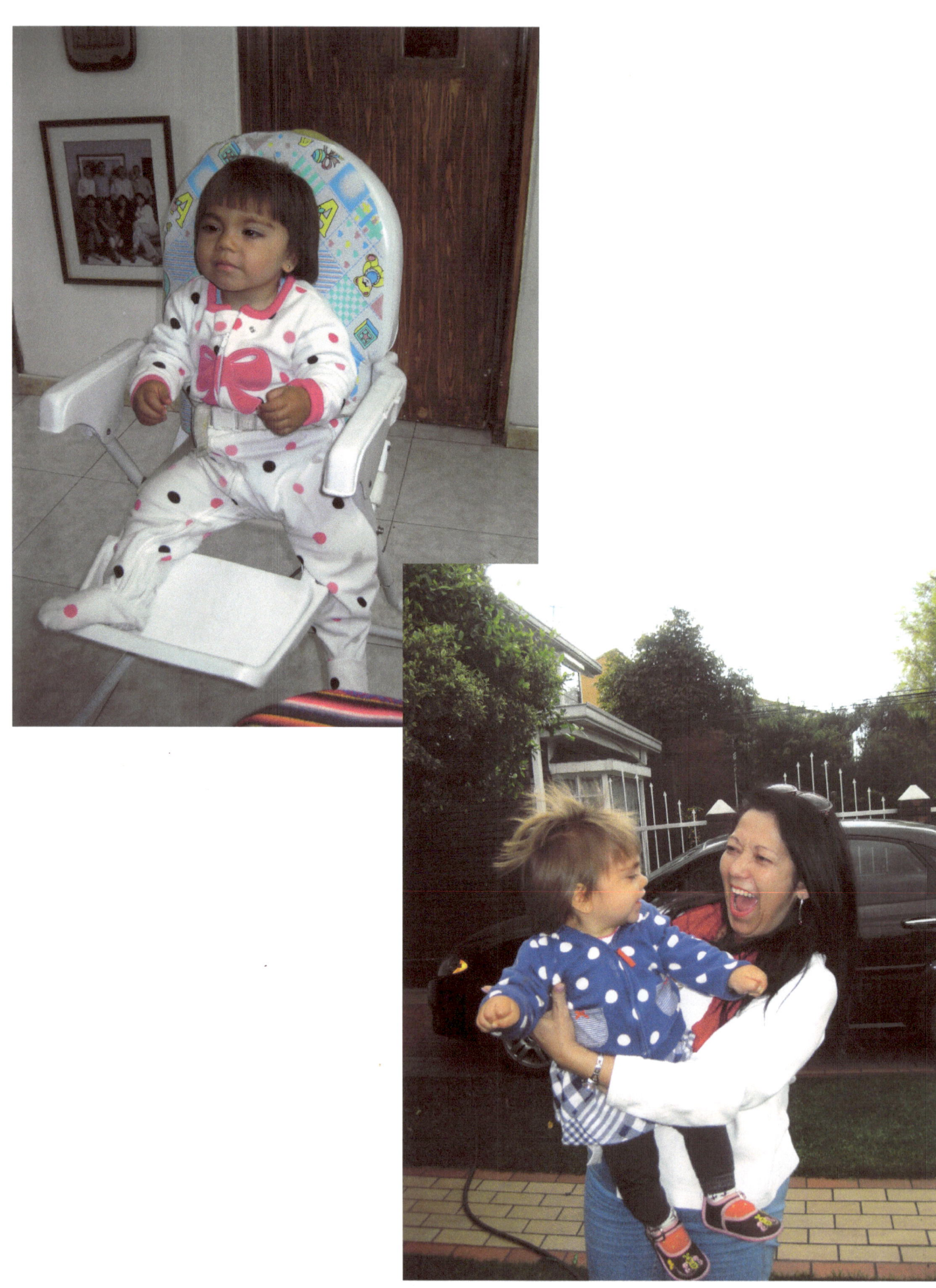

www.ingramcontent.com/pod-product-compliance
Lightning Source LLC
Chambersburg PA
CBHW050355180526
45159CB00005B/2031